PUBLISHED by PARABLES
Earthly Stories with a Heavenly Meaning

THE MYSTERY OF FASTING

By
NATHANIEL MCNEIL

PUBLISHED by PARABLES
Earthly Stories with a Heavenly Meaning

The Mystery of Fasting
Nathaniel McNeil

Published By Parables
June , 2019

All Rights Reserved. No part of this book may be reproduced or utilized in any form or by any means, electronic or mechanical, including photocopying, recording, or by any information storage and retrieval system, without permission in writing from the author.

ISBN **978-1-945698-91-0**
Printed in the United States of America

Readers should be aware that Internet Web sites offered as citations and/or sources for further information may have been changed or disappeared between the time this was written and the time it is read.

THE MYSTERY OF FASTING

By
NATHANIEL MCNEIL

For speaking engagements, conferences, revivals and seminars contact Nathaniel mcneil by email at bishopnmcneil@icloud .com

The Mystery of Fasting

CONTENTS

ACKNOWLEDGEMENTS	3
INTRODUCTION	5
The Purpose of Fasting	7
Unveiling the True Meaning of	25
Biblical Examples of Fasting and Consecration	35
Fasting Revelations from the Bible	49
Uncovering the Bridegroom's Fast	53
The Rewards of Fasting	63
Supernatural Laws of Fasting	91
Faith We Will Need in Our Fasting	99
How to Fast	107
Manifestations of the Sons of God	139
CONCLUSION	144

Nathaniel McNeil

The Mystery of Fasting
ACKNOWLEDGEMENTS

I would like to dedicate this book to my late grandmother and overseer Rosa A. James. Who always believed in me even as a child. My father the late Bishop Nathaniel McNeil Sr., who passed the spiritual legacy on to me. His words of wisdom still speak to me as I continue to learn.

I want to thank Sister Joann Hicks for her tireless work, sleepless nights and effort in helping me to get this book out. Your heart for ministry and your passion for Christ will always be remembered by me and rewarded by Christ. To Christine Gordon and Willie Mae Harris, your faith in the vision, love for the ministry and financial support in which I cannot thank you enough. Archbishop Chris Christian, who stood with me through the great storms of my life as a good spiritual son but also as a brother in Christ. Dr. Brian Mosley, a spiritual leader and father who gave direction, guidance and counsel. I appreciate you from my heart. Jacqueline Lawrence, for her love, loyalty, faithfulness and her prayer team for their ceaseless prayers for me. I thank you. I am grateful to Regina Peet for her friendship, support and encouragement during my ups and downs. Also, a great mention for Bishop P. F. Chambers, as this book would not be possible without all the help of the above mentioned.

To Kassandra Dixon who labored with me in preparing my manuscripts, proofreading, praying with me and encouraging me to complete this book. I appreciate you.

Finally, to my mother Elect Lady Vivian McNeil, who taught me how to read, and gave me my first book, instructed me on how to fight and persevere. Even now these are the tools that I use. I am more grateful to you than you will ever know.

Bishop Nathaniel McNeil

Nathaniel McNeil

INTRODUCTION
What is Fasting?

The Mystery of Fasting

The word "fast" itself gives us a clue. By avoiding food or certain types of food for a time, we literally speed up the natural detoxification and cleansing process that is happening constantly in our body and we speed up cellular renewal and regeneration. Thus, a fast is a cure, a remedy, and a therapeutic action. In the purest sense of the word, fasting refers to a total abstinence from all food, whether it's for forty days, ten days or just one day. In more modern times, fasting can also refer to the limiting of eating certain foods or perhaps eating only one type of food or taking fresh fruit and vegetable juices only. There are so many different types of fasts and forms of internal cleansings to choose from and you can tailor them to suit your individual needs. You can even do a simple cleansing by avoiding all alcohol, dairy, caffeine, and processed food and drinking more water if you like, this alone will have an extremely beneficial effect on your body.

Biblical Fasting

A fast is a highly focused time when we examine our lives and seek to align ourselves with the ways of God. We do this by separating ourselves from our typical patterns and routines and entering a spiritual experience for a given time. Fasting is a spiritual discipline, and the practice has tenets that we want to follow so we can be assured of a successful experience. God has instructed us on how to fast and the attitude to have when fasting. Thus, true fasting is to be practiced. We are in the time of fasting. Fasting is walking in the spirit to the highest degree. Understand that fasting isn't to abuse the flesh but to advance in the spirit realm. We are crucifying the flesh because the things of the flesh will die. You must strive to walk like a person of the spirit rather than the flesh. The demons don't want this. They don't want you to access advancement into the spirit and obtain the power to control them to walk in your God-given destiny. Thus, there will be a conflict between your determination and your flesh because when you attempt to spiritualize the body, the flesh will fight it. You may have a headache, feel dizzy, or nauseated.

Skipping food for an entire day is an even bigger victory for many. Going two days or more without food can be like a "Medal of Honor" status! Anyone that knows anything about fasting will tell you to start safely and conservatively and build up a history of victories which, over time, you can look back on and build your confidence while going into a new fast. Fasting is temporary, which means it is doable. Even lifelong meat lovers can practice the Daniel's consecration as Scriptures place it and go without meat for just twenty-one days. Setting aside a specific and limited amount of time for fasting sharpens our focus on God. We then can enter more deeply into His truths. As we open our hearts to the Holy Spirit and purpose ourselves to learn from Him, our Father can minister to us as His precious children.

Prayer and fasting often go hand in hand, but this is not always the case. You can pray without fasting but cannot fast without praying. It is when these two activities are combined and dedicated to God's glory that they reach their full effectiveness. Having a dedicated time of prayer and fasting is not a way of manipulating God into doing what you desire. Instead, it is simply forcing yourself to focus and rely on God for the strength, provision, and wisdom you need.

1

THE PURPOSE OF FASTING

As a little boy growing up in Brooklyn, New York, I was the son of a pastor. I saw many pastors and ministers that operated in the power of God. I did not fully understand how they got there---it was a mystery to me. One thing that I knew, for sure, was that there was a call on my life and that someday, I would minister under His power. At age 19, I became interested in the power of fasting. I felt the leading, of God, to fast but I was fearful. I really wanted to live for God, to take on his character and to be able to work in His power. I was greatly impacted by the book, ***Atomic Power with God by Fasting and Prayer***, by Dr. Franklin Hall. One day, I boldly announced to my father, "Daddy, I am going on my first extended fast for forty days and it is going to be a water fast." He looked at me and he knew that I was serious. I was serious and I was on fire! All day I was excited and rejoicing in what God was going to do in me and through me---until I ate those two Twinkies. I was feeling a bit disappointed, but I knew that I had to try again. Five or six days later I tried again. As a result of the extended fast, I realized that I had laser-focus and had become far more sensitive to hearing God. As I continued in ministry, I made fasting a part of my toolbox. I would fast from 7-50 days. As a young man, in my early 20s, I traveled across the country preaching the gospel. I saw the manifestations of fasting: healing, deliverance and miracles. In my first church, as a pastor, we went from 6 people to over 300 people within several weeks. We saw people get saved, healed, and delivered.

There are powers and demons assigned to take your inheritance, reel you into unhealthy relationships and keep you hurt about the past. The spiritual power we experience through fasting is a mystery. Fasting is a mystery—I can't tell you why it works, but I can tell you that it works. It is a law of the spirit because fasting is a mystery given to us by God to access the powers of the world to come and the dominion of God. What are mysteries? There are some things beyond the understanding of the natural. A mystery is known by revelation and not fully understood in the natural. We can't understand how it works because it simply defies explanation. The mysteries of God are his hidden secret things only given to those who are born again.

In the Bible, the term *"mystery"* refers specifically to insights and truths we understand when God reveals them directly to our spirit. When we fast, we fully surrender ourselves to the spirit of God, soul and body. We submit our will to God, follow a set of guidelines about food, and open our hearts to this mystery. God miraculously uses our submission to strengthen us, empower us, fill us, and change us. We get a taste of what Jesus meant when He said, you are in me, and I am in you (John 14:20). When we fast, we focus more of our attention on God through prayer and study. These mysteries are not for everyone. Only those of the dominion or rule of God will be made aware by God. ***"But we speak the wisdom of God in a mystery, [G3466] even the hidden wisdom, which God ordained before the world unto our glory"*** (1 Corinthians 2:7). ***"Let a man so account of us, as of the ministers of Christ, and stewards of the mysteries [G3466] of God"*** (1 Corinthians 4: 1). Fasting is a mystery instrument of blessing to access this realm of miracles in the spirit. The truth is, fasting is for today! Now more than ever! The combination of fasting and praying is not a fad or a novelty approach to spiritual discipline. Fasting and praying are not part of a human-engineered method or plan, and they are not the means to manipulate a situation or to create a circumstance. Fasting and praying are Bible-based disciplines that are appropriate for all believers of all ages throughout all centuries in all parts of the world.

Through the years, I have learned that many people in the church have never been taught about fasting and prayer, and many have therefore never fasted and prayed. As a result, they don't know why fasting and praying are important, what the Bible teaches about fasting, or how to fast. To many, fasting sounds like drudgery—or a form of religious works. To others, fasting sounds extremely difficult. People tend to stand in awe at reports of those who have fasted for several weeks. When I hear about such

The Mystery of Fasting

fasting, I no doubt think what they think: If I fasted that long, I'd die! I couldn't possibly do that!

Let me assure you at the outset of this book that I am not advocating prolonged periods of fasting for every believer. A fast can be as short as one meal. Neither do I advocate fasting nor praying for the mere sake of saying with self-righteousness, "I have fasted and prayed about this." I do not advocate fasting so that the hungry in a foreign nation might have the food you would have eaten that day—which is highly unlikely. I do not advocate fasting apart from prayer.

There are mysteries of the spirit realm that are practiced in the spirit realm to oppose your healing, deliverance and breakthrough to manifested prayers.

"And the LORD said unto Moses, See, I have made thee a God to Pharaoh: and Aaron thy brother shall be thy prophet" (Exodus 7:1). God tells Moses, that he is a God to Pharaoh. But how? By Aaron speaking and doing what he told him to do. Pharaoh represents the world powers. *"And the LORD spoke unto Moses and Aaron, saying, When Pharaoh shall speak unto you, saying," 'Show a miracle for you: then thou shalt say unto Aaron, Take thy rod, and cast it before Pharaoh, and it shall become a serpent. And Moses and Aaron went in unto Pharaoh, and they did so as the LORD had commanded: and Aaron cast down his rod before Pharaoh, and before his servants, and it became a serpent. Then Pharaoh also called the wise men and the sorcerers: now the magicians of Egypt, they also did in like manner with their enchantments. For they cast down every man his rod, and they became serpents: but Aaron's rod swallowed up their rods"* (Exodus 7:8-12).

Notice: he opposes Moses by using sorcery—operating by demons in the spirit realm. But Moses can overcome this by obeying the Word of God. There are mysteries of the spirit realm that is known to the world in high places to achieve the goals and purpose of Satan. 2 Kings 6:3-8 said: "And one said, be content, I pray thee, and go with thy servants." And he answered, "I will go." So, he went with them. And when they came to Jordan, they cut down wood. But as one was felling a beam, the ax head fell into the water: and he cried, and said, "Alas, master! For it was borrowed." And the man of God said, "Where fell it?" And he showed him the place. And he cut down a stick, and cast it in thither, and the iron did swim. Therefore, said he, "Take it up to thee." And he put out his hand and took it." Elisha understood mysteries with which to get results manifested in the natural realm. It's a mystery how a stick could find and retrieve an iron, but it did.

Throughout this teaching, I have sprinkled various reasons for you to fast. These are all important and will produce in your life as you learn how to fast and when God is prompting you to fast. To choose a definition that can inspire you to live a fasted life, it would be that fasting is the destruction of fleshly desires through the denial of food. It gives you power over the influences of the world that feeds your carnal nature and makes you subject to what your flesh wants instead of what God wants.

I've shared God's purpose in fasting for: personal breakthroughs, to be free from sin; for repentance; for God's protection; God's direction and among others, God's guidance. However, God wants you to go from fasting for personal purposes and mature to where you fast for His purposes.

Unless God calls you to a specific fast for a specific purpose, the overall purposes of God in fasting is outlined in Isaiah chapter 58. Purpose is defined as: something set up as an object or end to be attained. Purpose is God's goal for you in fasting. It's what He eventually expects from His people as they draw closer to Him and mature in the things of the Lord.

Isaiah 58:1 says:

[1]   "Cry aloud, spare not; Lift up your voice like a trumpet; Tell My people their transgression, and the house of Jacob their sins.

[2]   Yet they seek Me daily, and delight to know My ways, as a nation that did righteousness, and did not forsake the ordinance of their God. They ask of Me the ordinances of justice; They take delight in approaching God.

[3]   Why have we fasted,' they say, ˜and You have not seen? Why have we afflicted our souls, and You take no notice?' "In fact, in the day of your fast you find pleasure, and exploit all your laborers.

The Mystery of Fasting

[4]   Indeed, you fast for strife and debate, And to strike with the fist of wickedness. You will not fast as you do this day, to make your voice heard on high.

[5]   Is it a fast that I have chosen, a day for a man to afflict his soul? Is it to bow down his head like a bulrush, and to spread out sackcloth and ashes? Would you call this a fast, and an acceptable day to the Lord?

[6]   Is this not the fast that I have chosen: To loose the bonds of wickedness, to undo the heavy burdens, to let the oppressed go free, And that you break every yoke?

[7]   Is it not to share your bread with the hungry, And that you bring to your house the poor who are cast out; When you see the naked, that you cover him, And not hide yourself from your own flesh?

[8]   Then your light shall break forth like the morning, Your healing shall spring forth speedily, and your righteousness shall go before you; the glory of the Lord shall be your rear guard.

[9]   Then you shall call, and the Lord will answer; You shall cry, and He will say, ˜Here I am.' "If you take away the yoke from your midst, the pointing of the finger, and speaking wickedness,

[10]   If you extend your soul to the hungry and satisfy the afflicted soul, then your light shall dawn in the darkness, and your darkness shall be as the noonday.

[11]   The Lord will guide you continually, and satisfy your soul in drought, and strengthen your bones; you shall be like a watered garden, and like a spring of water, whose waters do not fail.

[12]   Those from among you shall build the old waste places; you shall raise up the foundations of many generations; and you shall be called the Repairer of the Breach, The Restorer of Streets to Dwell In.

[13]   "If you turn away your foot from the Sabbath, From doing your pleasure on My holy day, And call the Sabbath a delight, The holy day of the Lord honorable, And shall honor Him, not doing your own ways, Nor finding your own pleasure, Nor speaking your own words,

[14]   Then you shall delight yourself in the Lord; and I will cause you to ride on the high hills of the earth and feed you with the heritage of Jacob your father. The mouth of the Lord has spoken.

In looking at what transpires in this passage of Scripture, this chapter contains a severe rebuke of the Jews on account of their hypocrisy in practicing and relying on outward ceremonies, such as fasting and bodily humiliation, without true repentance.

As God reveals His heart in this manner, He sets the stage for something that Jesus would say as He addressed the religious leaders of His day.

In Matthew chapter 15, Jesus reveals the motives of the scribes and Pharisees and upsets them by answering this question in a manner that offended them. Verse 2 begins:

"[2] Why do Your disciples transgress the tradition of the elders? For they do not wash their hands when they eat bread.

[3]   He answered and said to them, "Why do you also transgress the commandment of God because of your tradition?

[4]   For God commanded, saying, honor your father and your mother'; and, He who curses father or mother, let him be put to death.' [

5] But you say, Whoever says to his father or mother, "Whatever profit you might have received from me is a gift to God "

[6] then he need not honor his father or mother.' Thus you have made the commandment of God of no effect by your tradition.

[7] Hypocrites! Well did Isaiah prophesy about you, saying:

[8] These people draw near to Me with their mouth, And honor Me with their lips, But their heart is far from Me.

[9] And in vain they worship Me, Teaching as doctrines the commandments of men.'

Jesus knew that the practice of our faith goes much deeper than what is seen through outward ceremonies. It's a matter of the heart that expresses itself in acts of obedience to the moral and ceremonial laws of God, not just having a desire to do them. Having a desire to do what is right does not equal obedience. Ironically, it's disobedience to know what is right and not do it and a person that knowingly disobeys God cannot expect to receive from Him. The traditions of men that were handed down from previous leaders and generations infiltrated the teachings that were supposed to be based on God's moral and ceremonial laws. Because of this, the Word of God was void of God's intended power to achieve what it was initially sent to perform. This generation transgressed or went beyond the boundaries God set around His Word, so that they could hold on to the traditions of men that had no ability to bring them closer to the Lord. This is what prompted the Lord's question in verse 3 saying, "Why do you also transgress the commandment of God because of your tradition?" The laws that were man-made eventually superseded the laws that God intended to rule the hearts and lives of the people. Therefore, the leaders and people alike were deceived and became hypocrites when it came to the things that pertained to God.

For these leaders to deceive the masses of people, they had to mingle religious terminology in with the things that were now customary for them during their gatherings. Therefore, the love they proclaimed they had for God was not demonstrated in what they did, only in what they said they would do.

Jesus also pointed this out in verse 7 saying, *"[7] Hypocrites! Well did Isaiah prophesy about you, saying: [8] These people draw near to Me with their mouth, And honor Me with their lips, But their heart is far from Me. [9] And in vain they worship Me, Teaching as doctrines the commandments of men.'*

In like manner, here in our text in Isaiah 58, verse 2 says, *"Yet they seek Me daily, and delight to know My ways, as a nation that did righteousness, and did not forsake the ordinance of their God. They ask of Me the ordinances of justice; They take delight in approaching God."* These people also had a religious fast when they approached the Lord. They had the time to meet with Him and said they wanted to do what pleased Him. However, they were compared to those who did what was right and were doing what God commanded. Yet they fell short of pleasing God. The first five verses in Isaiah chapter 58 clearly display the fact that you can be doing outward acts and have your heart far from God. These people clearly had wrong motives in doing "religious things. They were fasting for selfish gain and had turned God's time of fasting into times when they would feast instead of utilizing those times for the purposes of God. The second part of Verse 3 says, *"In fact, in the day of your fast you find pleasure, and exploit all your laborers. Indeed, you fast for strife and debate, And to strike with the fist of wickedness."*

God's people had turned times of fasting into holidays, and some would even disregard the most sacred fast by forcing their servants to work all day long. Others used fast days for the purpose of settling their accounts, posting up their books, and drawing out their bills to be ready to collect their debts. These were sneaking hypocrites; the others were daringly irreligious. As verse 4 says, they would fast for strife and debate, and to strike with the fist of wickedness.

This is important to see. There are some people who fast in order to get their own way as the word strife means, "a bitter sometimes violent conflict or dissension; to fight and struggle; an effort or argument for superiority." There are some people who will try to usurp the authority of the church and begin fasting in order that they would gain a certain office or position. This will play out in how they relate to the pastors and leadership as they promote themselves and put down those who are in leadership.

They will sow strife in the ministry and feel that their sole mission in life is to debate those who do their best to establish the purposes of
God.

Then there are people that fast in order that they would have victory while at war. Generally, you don't question this as if you're the nation going to war, you want your sons and daughters, husbands and fathers to be protected and return with a certain level of victory. However, the fact is, we cannot fast and ask God's blessing on wars that are carried on for the purposes of wrath and personal ambition. An example of this would be Alexander the Great and Adolph Hitler. In 1933, Hitler initiated polices to rid the Aryan race of undesirable elements and eliminate other races that he considered inferior and dangerous to the Germans. Alexander the Great was the king of Macedonia and conquered the Persian Empire in 335 B.C. He set himself up as a God shortly before he died and, after his death, his rise to deity was nullified by the people. These are two examples of people that

The Mystery of Fasting

carried out purposes for war based on wrath and personal ambition. Although extreme cases, these are fasts that cannot expect the hand of God to bless them.

Then Isaiah 58:6 begins sharing with us the type of fast that God does receive. It says, **"[6] Is this not the fast that I have chosen: To loose the bonds of wickedness, to undo the heavy burdens, to let the oppressed go free, and that you break every yoke? [7] Is it not to share your bread with the hungry, And that you bring to your house the poor who are cast out; When you see the naked, that you cover him, And not hide yourself from your own flesh?"**

As God begins asking the question of the type of fast that's pleasing to Him, He uses a word that's important in the Hebrew language. This word is "chosen".

Often when we associate the word chosen, especially in the New Testament, we refer to that which is hand-picked and chosen out from among many choices. However, this is very different. As God says that this is the type of fast that He has chosen. He refers to the fact that this is a fast that's been proven and therefore acceptable in His sight as accomplishing His purposes in the earth. The Hebrew word is, Bachar and means "to prove, try, choose, select, distinguish, love, like, to be pleasing, to be especially chosen." Something is acceptable or judged to be excellent after it has been tested. In other words, it is the best. This word involves a careful, well thought out choice.

Choosing as used here involves taking a keen look at something as Isaiah 48:10 in the KJV says, **"Behold, I have refined thee, but not with silver. I have chosen thee in the furnace of affliction."** God is saying there, that you have not come to salvation by accident. After you've been tried in the furnace of life and even thought you were left for dead with no one else to turn to and appearing like no one else wanted you, God says, He did and He views you as being excellent and the very best there is to accomplish His purposes.

In like manner, God is saying that the type of fast that He reveals here is acceptable and has been judged to be exceptional in His sight.

This is a fast for those who come to a place of maturity as it forsakes the benefits of fasting for your own purposes and embraces the greater purposes of God.

Isaiah 58 reveals an *"eight-fold fast. There are eight components to it and although you may be led to certain portions of this on any specific occasion, the goal is to find out what God desires and follow the leading of the Holy Spirit."*

Verse 6 says, *"To loose the bonds of wickedness, to undo the heavy burdens, to let the oppressed go free, and that you break every yoke?"*

There are bands of wickedness that have many people bound; people walking around with heavy burdens and oppressed and under the yoke of slavery to the devil. This is the first thing the Lord wants to get off those who are called to salvation.

People with addictive behaviors such as alcoholism and drugs; those that have a controlling spirit; those with sexual addictions; habitual liars and thieves as well as many more addictions; all need people in their lives who will lay down their own lives by fasting that they would be loosed from these things.

They may never meet you or even know you by name; however, your obedience to God in this area will bring great deliverance to multitudes.

What must be realized is that bondages come in all shapes, colors and cultures. Bondage is the inability to control yourself when compelled to do what is wrong. You are mastered by someone or something other than God. There are people in bondage that you can fast specifically for. You can have a friend or loved one that is constantly bound by pornography or homosexuality, rebellion, and failure. God has given us the great privilege of knowing that no one is beyond hope and laying down your life for them by fasting, not only delivers them but also, brings them to the point of salvation.

Verse 6 deals with the spiritual things that come against a person's life and verse 7 allows you to see that there are natural things that must be done as well.

These are acts of love that are demonstrated by what we do, and not what we say. This is why James told us to put works to our words. This verse is likened to James 2:14 which says:

The Mystery of Fasting

"[14] What does it profit, my brethren, if someone says he has faith but does not have works? Can faith save him? [15] If a brother or sister is naked and destitute of daily food, [16] and one of you says to them, "Depart in peace, be warmed and filled, but you do not give them the things which are needed for the body, what does it profit? [17] Thus also faith by itself, if it does not have works, is dead. [18] But someone will say, "You have faith, and I have works. Show me your faith without your works, and I will show you my faith by my works."

Isaiah 58:7 is the scripture that upholds what James is saying in our New Testament. First, you're to provide food for those that lack. Your fast should include looking for opportunities to give to those who are hungry. Even if it is in proportion to what you are going without, you should look at how you can bless someone else with their natural nourishment. Notice, it says that you share your bread. The person who will do this is opportunistic. They are looking for opportunities to share what they would have eaten with someone else who may be lacking. This could include helping a national and international feeding ministry such as Feed the Children or locally by helping someone you know that is in need or our local mission. This is the true fast, to break your bread with the hungry, breaking bread on purpose for them, giving them loaves and not to put them off with scraps or what is going rotten in your refrigerator. The same principle holds true for the other things listed beginning with providing shelter for the wanderer and clothes for those that lack. Especially in today's society, we must be careful in bringing just anyone into our home. We have local shelters for both men and women that provide for strangers and will clothe them, feed them, and give them shelter. However, we must also be sensitive to and embrace opportunities that present themselves with people we know. You must be careful as single people to not let someone of the opposite sex into your home and if you have young children, you also must make certain you don't open them up to physical, sexual, or mental abuse. Hebrews 13:2 tells us *"Do not forget to entertain strangers, for by so doing some have unwittingly entertained angels."* Jesus also said, *"I was a stranger and you took me in."*

Unless you know exactly what God is saying, you must use wisdom for the hour in which we live and ensure that these people are taken care of. The Good Samaritan found the man beaten on the road, fixed his wounds, and then paid for him to be taken care of at a local motel. You must know what God is specifically speaking to you.

Thirdly, to provide clothing for those that want it: "When thou see the naked, cover him," both to shelter him from the weather and to enable him to appear decently among his neighbors.

If he or she desires such, give him or her clothes to come to church in, go to school in or go to work in. If you do give, please give things that are wearable. Don't give things that have holes in them or are dirty. Let those who receive your clothes have a sense of dignity in wearing them. Also, don't give them and then look for them. Your responsibility is to obey God and what is done with them is God's responsibility.

KEY REASONS TO FAST

I encourage every believer to fast for two significant reasons:

1. The Scriptures Teach Us to Fast

The Bible has a great deal to say about fasting, including commands to fast. The Bible also gives us examples of people who fasted, using different types of fasts for various reasons, all of which had very positive results. Jesus fasted. Jesus' disciples fasted after the Resurrection. Many of the Old Testament heroes and heroines of the faith fasted. The followers of John the Baptist fasted. Many people in the early church fasted. What the Scriptures have taught us directly and by the examples of the saints is undoubtedly something we are to do.

2. Fasting Puts You in the Best Possible Position for a Breakthrough

Fasting is the way to access the deeper things of God. That breakthrough might be in the realm of the spirit. It may be in the realm of your emotions or personal habits. It may be in the realm of a convenient area of life, such as a relationship or finances. What I have seen repeatedly through the years—not only in the Scriptures but in countless personal stories that others have told me—is that periods of fasting produces great spiritual results, many of which fall into the realm of a breakthrough. What was not a reality suddenly becomes a reality because what had not worked---suddenly did. The unwanted situation or object that was there suddenly was not there. The relationship that was unlovable was suddenly loved. The job that had not materialized suddenly did. The straightforward and direct conclusions I draw are these: First, if the Bible teaches us to do something, I want to do it. I want to obey the Lord in every way that He commands me to obey Him. And second, if fasting is a means to a breakthrough that God has for me, I want to undertake those disciplines so that I might experience that breakthrough!

Every person that I know needs a breakthrough in some area of his or her life. I am no exception. I need breakthroughs all the time—it may be a breakthrough in understanding a situation, an advance answer to a problem, a breakthrough idea, a breakthrough insight, a discovery in the financial or material provision, a breakthrough in health. If you have any need in your life, you need a breakthrough from God to meet that need! Fasting breaks the yoke of bondage and brings about a release of God's presence, power, and provision.

The breakthrough that you may need in your life is a sense of God's direction—not only for today and tomorrow, but the broad scope of your life. If you long to know God's purpose for you on this earth, I strongly encourage you to seek God in fasting.

WHAT DOES FASTING ACCOMPLISH?

Spending time in prayer and fasting is not automatically effective in accomplishing the desires of those who fast. Fasting or no fasting, God only promises to answer our prayers when we ask according to His will. 1 John 5:14-15 tells us, "This is the confidence we have in approaching God: that if we ask anything according to His will, He hears us. And if we know that He hears us - whatever we ask - we know that we have what we asked of Him." In the prophet Isaiah's time, the people grumbled that they had fasted, yet God did not answer in the way they wanted (Isaiah 58:3-4). Isaiah responded by proclaiming that the external show of fasting, without the proper heart attitude, was futile (Isaiah 58:5-9).

How do you know if you are praying and fasting according to God's will? Are you praying and fasting for things that honor and glorify God? Does the Bible reveal that it is God's will for you? If we are asking for something that is not honoring to God or not God's will for our lives, God will not give what we ask for, whether we fast or not. How can we know God's will? God promises to give us wisdom when we pray. James 1:5 tells us, "If any of you lack wisdom, he should ask God, who gives generously to all without finding fault, and it will be given to him."

FASTING – IS IT REQUIRED OR RECOMMENDED?

The Mystery of Fasting

The Word of God REQUIRES believers to spend time in Fasting. Fasting is something we should be doing. Far too often, though, the focus of fasting is on abstaining from food. Instead, the purpose of Christian fasting should be to take our eyes off the things of this world and focus our thoughts on God. fasting should always be limited to a set time because not eating for extended periods can be damaging to the body. Fasting is not a method of punishing our bodies, and it is not to be used as a "dieting method" either. We are not to spend time fasting to lose weight, but rather to gain a deeper fellowship with God.

By taking our eyes off the things of this world through Biblical fasting, we can focus better on Christ. Matthew 6:16-18 declares, "When you fast, do not look somber as the hypocrites do, for they disfigure their faces to show men they are fasting. I tell you the truth; they have received their reward in full. But when you fast, put oil on your head and wash your face, so that it will not be obvious to men that you are fasting, but only to your Father, who is unseen; and your Father, who sees what is done in secret, will reward you."

One can pray without fasting, but you cannot fast authentically without praying.

Without this spiritual dimension, the twenty-one-day consecration/mourning of Daniel, which some refer to as the Daniel fast, would be no different than a typical diet. Many believe that Daniel was on a fast, however, scriptures reveal that Daniel was not fasting, he mourned and afflicted himself. Which is different from fasting, but can also bring great results. The correct term is 'Daniel mourned' or 'Daniel afflicted himself for twenty-one-days'.

But since this is first a spiritual experience made to draw us closer to God, we aren't dieting. Instead, we are placing ourselves into holy submission. When on a diet, we might occasionally cheat or fail to keep the promises we made to ourselves. But a fast is different. Because when we fast, we are merging with God for a spiritual outcome. We are expecting Him to impact our lives, so we maintain our commitment to Him. Here's another difference: When God's Spirit empowers our spirit, we experience His support and become steadfast in our commitment. Suddenly we have the power and the desire to say no to things not allowed on the fast. Our motivation to succeed becomes so much stronger than the temptation to drink a can of soda or eat a slice of pizza. This new-found discipline is part of the compelling mystery of fasting.

For many, the demands of everyday life are so packed with activities, responsibilities, and to-do lists that feeling overwhelmed is normal. With so many pressures, few have time to feed their soul. The result is spiritual and emotional starvation, a deep inner hunger for peace, rest, and security. And this hunger is pervasive. At every age, in every walk of life, too many of us are starving for the nourishment that only God can provide.

When we fast, we come to the Lord's table and feast on His love, care, and wisdom. We change our behavior. We slow our pace. We focus intently on spiritual matters and enjoy what our souls are truly hungry for—Jesus, the Bread of Life. Unfortunately, too many of us try to satisfy our hunger with the spiritual equivalent of fast food, self-defeating behaviors, relationships that have more to do with feeding carnal hunger than the longing of the soul. Author and Pastor John Piper writes, "Do you have a hunger for God? If we don't feel strong desires for the manifestation of the glory of God, it is not because we have drunk deeply and are satisfied. It is because we have nibbled so long at the table of the world. Our soul is stuffed with small things, and there is no room for the great. If we are full of what the world offers, then perhaps a fast might express, or even increase, our soul's appetite for God. Between the dangers of self-denial and self-indulgence is the path of pleasant pain called fasting." Indeed, the call deep within us beckons not for natural food or pleasures. What our souls are truly hungry for is the Bread of Life of the Lord who said, *"People do not live by bread alone"* (Matthew 4:4). And Jesus responds to our hunger with this invitation:

"Come to Me, all you who are weary and burdened, and I will give you rest. Take My yoke upon you and learn from Me, for I am gentle and humble in heart, and you will find rest for your souls" (Matthew 11:28- 29).

The Mystery of Fasting

2

UNVEILING THE TRUE MEANING OF PRAYER

What is prayer and why is it so important? How many people go to church and have been in church but have no idea what prayer is and how to do it?
To get answers, we must be taught to pray, that's right: taught to pray properly. Because, truly, it isn't just about asking for things. It is much deeper than that.

The Mystery of Fasting

And when thou prayest, thou shalt not be as the hypocrites are: for they love to pray standing in the synagogues and in the corners of the streets, that they may be seen of men. Verily I say unto you, they have their reward [6] but thou, when thou prayest, enter into thy closet, and when thou hast shut thy door, pray to thy father which is in secret; and thy father which seeth in secret shall reward thee openly.

[7]But when ye pray, use not vain repetitions, as the heathen do: for they think that they shall be heard for their much speaking" (Matthew 6:5-7). We have heard some powerful words of elegance and mastery of usage, but is this prayer? Is this what God constituted as prayer?

[8] Here in Matthew 6, Jesus works on the motives for prayer before giving them the model of prayer.

Why? You search your motives in prayer before praying.
"be not ye therefore like unto them: for your father knoweth what things ye have need of, before ye ask him.
[9] After this manner therefore pray ye: our father which art in heaven, hallowed be thy name.
[10] Thy kingdom come. Thy will be done in earth, as it is in heaven.
[11] Give us this day our daily bread.
[12] And forgive us our debts, as we forgive our debtors.
[13] And lead us not into temptation but deliver us from evil: for thine is the kingdom, and the power, and the glory, forever. Amen.
[14] For if ye forgive men their trespasses, your heavenly father will also forgive you: [15]
But if ye forgive not men their trespasses, neither will your father forgive your trespasses" (Matthew 6:8-15).

This is not the Lord's prayer or even Jesus praying here, as most refer to this passage of scripture. But much deeper. After dealing with the correct heart and motives of prayer, now, God gives his disciples the model or outline on how to pray. This is not a prayer but an outline of how to pray. He was teaching to pray to reach and connect with God the father. Praying has definite rewards and is most essential in our lives. Prayer is so essential and important to God that Jesus takes the time to teach his disciples how to pray.

This ultimately means that man doesn't decide how to communicate with the creator who made him, but we are taught how to communicate with Him.

"ye ask, and receive not, because ye ask amiss, that ye may consume it upon your lusts" (James 4:3). The word amiss in Greek is kakos, which means improperly, wrongly.

This presumes God must hear us regardless of his instructions on how to approach him. I'm thinking of my mother who taught us respect for our elders. We were not allowed to just enter one of her conversations with grown-ups and ask her questions, not unless it was an emergency. This was good instruction for being mannerly.

The same goes with God, he teaches us how… now, there are emergencies that I am quite sure God knows. But when you are given the opportunity to develop relationship with him and you refuse to learn based on your own ideas, that is sin. The root of this "kakos" in Greek means not as we ought to be. It references the mode of thinking, feeling, and acting. It points to the character or lacking of character. God will not indulge you in your evil character. It is evil character to approach God based on how you think he should be handled. Improperly and wrongly means praying outside of the intended purpose, design, and meaning of prayer.

So, what exactly is prayer? Prayer in Hebrew is **tephillah**. It means intercession, entreaty, supplication, the root word of tephillah is **palal**.

Palal means to execute judgement, to mediate, judge, entreat. The Greek word for pray is **proseuchomi** which means to offer prayer to God.

The root words that make up this word gives us a much deeper meaning to what prayer really is. They mean —the Greek word *pros* —means to or at near, toward.

So, praying is to be directed at moving you toward, and nearing you to God. Thus, prayer moves you toward and near God. This word **alos** means—according to God.

So, prayers must be according to God. Prayer is the motions toward God and brings us near to according to God's will.

The Mystery of Fasting

We cannot just enter his presence and draw near without understanding how He instructs us to do this. ***Euchomai,*** the second root word means desires, feelings and inner will communicated to God. To express yourself. To confer your desires to God. And to express your will.

Desire stresses the strength of feeling and implies a strong aim. It is supplication. Supplication, though, isn't just making your request known to God but a bit deeper.

Supplication involves humility. It means to make yourself humble before God. It is earnest asking and communicating to God realizing who He is as the father.

Supplication is the posture of humility...

It is also urgent asking...

It means calling for immediate attention of God in humility.

We have the scripture that references us to come boldly to the throne of grace to obtain mercy...

Let's rightly divide this scripture through. This isn't coming to or busting up into heaven to the throne of God demanding him about our needs and what we want...

Let's look at Hebrews which speaks of boldly coming to God.

"[14] seeing then that we have a great high priest, that is passed into the heavens, Jesus the son of God, let us hold fast our profession [15] For we have not a high priest which cannot be touched with the feeling of our infirmities; but was in all points tempted like as we are, yet without sin.

[16] let us therefore come boldly unto the throne of grace, that we may obtain mercy, and find grace to help in time of need" (Hebrews 4:14-16).

The word boldly here in verse 16 is meta in the Greek.

Meta means in the midst of denoting union, being in God's presence before the throne.

It means being equipped to, among, or furnished to be among or in the midst. To magnify.

So, when we put this all together with verses 14 and 15, it is telling us that because Jesus Christ is our high priest that sits in heaven, the highest level of existence, but has experienced what it means to be mankind, he will be gracious when we come before the father. His blood makes it possible to come before the throne of the father. The righteousness of Christ equips us and furnishes us to come into the very midst, presence of the father...

Boldly then is the ability or privilege granted by the father to come in to his presence at the throne of grace because of the finished work of our high priest, Jesus Christ our lord.

Back to the Greek word euchomai, this word means to entreat God, which is an earnest request to overcome resistance. Who resists us? Satan and demonic forces.

It means we are of intense and serious state of mind.

Earnest also means that we can share humbly based on the word or guarantee which is his word of God to deal with this issue. We have a binding covenant sealed with the blood of Christ.

We use God's word in prayer not to remind him but to bind, cement, merge our request with his promise or inheritance he has given to us which seals the answer of the request made.

But how we come and in what attitude we approach God determines our ability to get into his presence.

Many have prayed outside the presence of the father but don't realize it. This is why Jesus taught his disciples how to pray.

Lastly, this word means to intercede. When most think of interceding, they think of praying for others which is partly true. But to intercede also means to reconcile your difference with God. God desires us to be reconciled, cleansed, or remove sin, better yet, repent.

It involves a repentant heart before whatever he brings or his searching of your heart. We must do self-examination.

So, let's recap!

What is prayer and praying? Pray means to beseech, implore God. Yes, it means to make your request known to him.

But greater than that we are commanded to pray.

Prayer is obedience to God first and foremost.

Why do we pray? Because God gave man authority on the earth and he will not invade it.

Man must invite God into his life and see him as who he is, the creator, by acknowledging that in prayer. We must invite God into our lives because we know and understand who he is.

Prayer establishes securely the law that we are giving it to God, and he will do it, not us. We are acknowledging him as our father and authority in our lives. We are inviting him to share in our desires and thoughts because our wellbeing and success relies on him.

It is acknowledging our dependency on him for all things. We must remind ourselves that God gave us life as a gift from him. He gave it to us.

When we pray, we are developing, and we increase in confidence that nothing is impossible because the father is with us.

Prayer helps us understand we are God's peculiar people.

Meaning we are his desire, protected, secure treasure of value and worth. It increases our understanding of our value and worth on earth.

Many are hurt, rejected etc. But prayer reminds us of our great importance to God who gave us life.

We develop security, in prayer. Many saints suffer from loneliness and insecurities due to lack of commitment to praying.

Prayer develops power, confidence, courage to face the unknown resistance in our lives.

Prayer shapes the success of our future.

Let's look at Jacob's ladder for a moment to see a visual of what prayer is doing.

"and he dreamed, and behold a ladder set up on the earth, and the top of it reached to heaven: and behold the angels of God ascending and descending on it" (Genesis 28:12).

This reveals that prayer connects earth with heaven. Same thing the book of Hebrews was saying when it said come boldly to the throne of grace… it's saying to connect with heaven from earth. Notice this ladder is set up on earth and it reaches to the heaven not the heavens. But the heaven. Satan's realm is in the heavens, but we have access to move beyond that realm and the authority that governs it. We have access to heaven, the holy of holies because we are Gods peculiar people, blood washed.

Our prayers are received of angels in the presence of God and they return with answers. These angels are going up and down with answers to prayers. When we pray, we are elevating ourselves from this earthly realm, this natural realm, physical realm and reaching the spirit realm.

When we look back at the Hebrew word for pray, the root of tefilah is palal which means to judge.
Prayer involves judging ourselves. It is self-examination.
It is the time of inward examination.
Prayer develops humility, when we realize we don't deserve God's hearing, but his mercy and the blood made it available to us.
We pray forgiveness and deliverance that we might mature.
When we self-examine ourselves according to the word, we ask for forgiveness and receive maturity.
Many are not mature in life because we fail to pray and examine ourselves before God.
'lord, help me to be a living epistle' was a term the old saints used in prayer.
Prayer is service.
The Hebrew word for service is **avodah.** It means service.
It means to serve God or make sacrifices of the heart through prayer.
Prayer is serving God with our hearts.
This sought of prayer purifies our minds, heart, desires, feelings, and character.
Service is work—we present our raw materials to God to mature and present us a finished product.
Praying is likened to a rough diamond in the coal mine. This rough diamond is discovered and made beautiful.
We are treasures of God, but prayer is what makes us beautiful and noticed.
God wants you to be noticed because it brings glory to his kingdom. I am stopping right here to prophesy that, for everyone who makes the decision to pray, that God cause you to be noticed and that you bring glory to his name. No more shame or being disregarded but you will be noticed! In the name of Jesus. God want you to be noticed!
Treasures are buried in the earth. Prayer digs in and pulls out the treasure. God wants to pull out of you everything that is beautiful and wonderful right now! Your earthen vessel carries tremendous treasure. Prayer pulls it out!

The Mystery of Fasting

Don't be jealous or envious of others but make the decision to pray. The spirit in prayer will make intercession for us.

"likewise, the spirit also helpeth our infirmities: for we know not what we should pray for as we ought: but the spirit itself maketh intercession for us with groanings which cannot be uttered. [27] And he that searcheth the hearts knoweth what is the mind of the spirit, because he maketh intercession for the saints according to the will of God" *(*romans 8:26).

The spirit's intercession is to purify, take away the impurities, cut, and polish us to be noticed in order to bring glory to God.

This intercession reaches in and pulls out our true God-given desires and your true self who God created. Many are products of environment, family hurts, pains, rejections, circumstances, hereditary conditions, and all that God created us to be is hidden beneath and covered by these hurts, pains, guards, facades we have built for our protection, poverty, sickness etc.

Prayer in this verse is the holy spirit who intercedes. It means he digs in and pulls it out of us. I prophesy now that as you pray from this day forward that God will dig deep and pull out of you who you really are. You don't have to go to etiquette school to be refined. Prayer is the refinery place of God. You think you are damaged goods. How many damaged goods saints are walking around? In fact, how many damaged goods thinking people are walking around today given the numerous counselors and shrinks? I say pray until God gets rid of the damage and presents the treasure in you. Damaged stems from the flesh.

When we are praying, it is our spirit that is getting stronger and stronger to overcome the flesh and manifest the treasure within us given by the God who created us.

I speak and prophesy now that this be a season of fasting for you. That you manifest the treasure God placed in you

So many materialistic souls today due to the lack of prayer. Our focus is money and material things. We chase money and material things of this world. But prayer makes us become balanced and centered on what is real. We gain a greater perspective on life and of life, thus, being made whole and healed.

There are way too many broken saints who can't minister effectively or do what God called them to do because they are so broken and bound by strongholds. Some accept it as the norm for their lives and abort their true purpose. When all that was needed was a fast.

Daily praying is a cleansing of our heart and souls to operate as a royal priesthood.

Prayer attaches us to God. Our spirits connect with his spirit. The breath of life in us is his spirit.

Our soul is the candle of life.

"for thou wilt light my candle: the lord my God will enlighten my darkness" (Psalm 18:28).

"the spirit of man is the candle of the lord, searching all the inward parts of the belly" (Proverbs 20:27).

Mankind has a natural longing for God. Our spirit longs to be connected to his spirit. It comes from his spirit. Even when it isn't realized. Drugs, inordinate sex, addiction, wrong relationships, anger, depression overeating etc. Are signs of longing for God. We attempt to replace the longing for our God-connection.

The fire of the soul is always moving upward even though we don't realize it, or should I say some may not realize it. Prayer then is the attaching of ourselves to God in Spirit to spirit connection. This is true fulfillment.

Praise is important in our fasting!

I won't go so deep into praise here, but I will say that praise is how we enter access to God.

Psalm 100:4—access to the throne is by thanking God. Not complaining. We must thank God for what he has already done, we must come before him with appreciation. Why? Because without seeing what he has already done we miss the understanding of who he is, and we don't relate our present breath of life and provision to his mercy and grace.

[[to the chief musician upon Gittith, a Psalm of David.]] *"[1] o lord our lord, how excellent is thy name in all the earth! Who hast set thy glory above the heavens. [2]*

The Mystery of Fasting

Out of the mouth of babes and sucklings hast thou ordained strength because of thine enemies, that thou mightest still the enemy and the avenger" (Psalm 8:1-2). Out of the mouth of babes.

In fasting, praise is paramount because you make large and exalt God by understanding the excellence of his name which are titles that reveal who He is. In other words, God is not a healer, he is healing!

He is above the heavens. Out of His throne proceeds the heavens. In fact, in him are all things made to exist.

Babes are fully dependent on Him for daily needs. This verse is powerful because it shares that God ordained praise because of our enemies and avengers. The word avengers in Hebrew denotes that whatever we have done that creates vengeances upon us. There are some things we have done that is due us hurt, and death... But praise will stop this curse... But it all comes from Satan. So, it's not just the enemy that comes against us but our own foolishness that comes back to haunt us. But praise will distill them both... Praise God!

Our praise paralyses the devil's evil spirit. Praise takes the sting out of the devil's opposition and he becomes weak. The devil's kryptonite is praise.

3

BIBLICAL EXAMPLES OF FASTING AND CONSECRATION

The Bible has many examples of individuals and entire nations going on a fast and consecration. These were generally called to further the purposes of God in a nation, as in the case of the consecration/mourning.

You can also look at the life of King David (2 Samuel 12:15-23) or the nation of Israel, as in the case of Josiah, (2 Kings chapters 21-23) to see that fasting and repentance are powerful forces that move the heart of the people while also moving obstacles out of the way of God's intended purposes.

However, there is an overlooked promise in the book of Isaiah that will serve the church well in the twenty-first century. After

The Mystery of Fasting

describing God's chosen fast, for those who will follow this prescribed model, chapter 58 ends with saying:
*"Then you shall delight yourself in the Lord; and I will cause you to ride on the high hills of the earth and feed you with the heritage of Jacob your father. The mouth of the Lord has spoken." This i*s a huge promise from God. He is saying that if you do things His way, He will feed you with something that's better than food and that is the heritage of Jacob.

A heritage is a birthright that you are to possess. Defined, it is "property that descends to an heir or an inheritance; something transmitted by or acquired from a predecessor; something possessed as a result of one's natural situation or birth." Furthermore, it is our heritage—heritage in the sense that it is an endowment belonging to us by ancient right from Abraham. This means our right to defeat Satan on earth is our inseparable inheritance given to us by God.

This power is in our domain. God assigns it because of His righteousness that we received when we were born again.

Fasting God's way and with His purposes as the thing that inspires you causes the actual transference of your birthright as a child of God into your life.

Seeing biblical examples of fasting, our greatest example of someone who fasted is Jesus Christ the Messiah. In this case you see that Jesus fasted to conquer Satan. If He had to do this as the Son of God, the same is true for us in this generation.

Although Jesus' life was filled with excitement, controversy, and miracles, there were two very significant events that preceded His going into public ministry.

One of these events was when He was baptized by John in the Jordan
River and the *"Holy Spirit descended in bodily form like a dove upon Him, and a voice came from heaven which said, You are My beloved Son; in You I am well pleased."* See: Luke 3:21, 22.

As great an event as this was, you would think it would have been the defining factor in Jesus' going forward to fulfill the purpose for which He was born. This was not the case; it's the ability to remain strong under the attacks of the enemy that qualifies you for public ministry. This is the second significant event that preceded Jesus going into public ministry.

In our generation, we are fascinated by those with strong anointing who can preach, teach, and pray. These are great gifts and are to be respected by all who are called to public ministry. However, the defining factor that qualifies a person for ministry is their ability to withstand the attacks of Satan without compromising the Word of God or compromising the moral standards that God expects from you as a child of God. You must be stable enough to withstand Satan as he attacks you with the intent to get you to compromise how you're supposed to live and what He has called you to do.

Luke 4 from verse 1 in the NKJV says:

"[1] Then Jesus, being filled with the Holy Spirit, returned from the Jordan and was led by the Spirit into the wilderness,

[2] being tempted for forty days by the devil. And in those days, He ate nothing, and afterward, when they had ended, He was hungry.

[3] And the devil said to Him, "If You are the Son of God, command this stone to become bread.

[4] But Jesus answered him, saying, "It is written, 'Man shall not live by bread alone, but by every word of God.'

[5] Then the devil, taking Him up on a high mountain, showed Him all the kingdoms of the world in a moment of time.

[6] And the devil said to Him, "All this authority I will give You, and their glory; for this has been delivered to me, and I give it to whomever I wish.

[7] Therefore, if You will worship before me, all will be Yours.

[8] And Jesus answered and said to him, "Get behind Me, Satan! For it is written, 'You shall worship the Lord your God, and Him only you shall serve.'

[9] Then he brought Him to Jerusalem, set Him on the pinnacle of the temple, and said to Him, "If You are the Son of God, throw Yourself down from here.

[10]   For it is written: 'He shall give His angels charge over you, To keep you,'

[11]   and, 'In their hands they shall bear you up, Lest you dash your foot against a stone.'

The Mystery of Fasting

[12]   And Jesus answered and said to him, "It has been said, 'You shall not tempt the Lord your God.'
[13]   Now when the devil had ended every temptation, he departed from Him until an opportune time.
[14]   Then Jesus returned in the power of the Spirit to Galilee, and news of Him went out through all the surrounding region"

What is noticeable here is the fact that Jesus did not only withstand the attacks of Satan, He did so at one of the weakest moments of His life—after He had fasted a long period of time. Extended fasting causes you to be physically weaker.

What Satan would have you focus on here is Jesus going without food for a long period of time and the temptations that were offered Him. However, the hidden fact that released Jesus was not that the Holy Spirit descended upon Him as we saw in Luke 3:21, 22. What released Jesus is that this same Holy Spirit empowered Him for what He would ultimately face as He pursued the Father's will. Jesus was born to die, and by dying, give life to everyone who would place their trust in Him.

Have you been empowered by the Holy Spirit for what you will ultimately face as you pursue the Father's will for your own life? Jesus didn't begin ministry until after He was baptized in water and until after the Holy Spirit entered or indwelled Him and until after He fasted for forty days. It was then that He was released into a powerful ministry with great signs, wonders, and miracles. We are supposed to do greater things than Jesus did, and this too shall become a reality before He returns to claim us as His bride. However, there must be a life of fasting before this will become a reality.

The Book of Daniel reveals that he consecrated on at least two occasions that were very significant. The first fast was to overcome his flesh while he received wisdom from God and the second was for a spiritual breakthrough.

Daniel 1 has him and the three Hebrew boys: Shadrach, Meshach, and Abednego living in Babylonian captivity. They were favored because of their purity and were educated and gifted mentally and spiritually. Daniel 1:

[3] Then the king ordered Ashpenaz, chief of his court officials, to bring in some of the Israelites from the royal family and the nobility

[4] young men without any physical defect, handsome, showing aptitude for every kind of learning, well informed, quick to understand, and qualified to serve in the king's palace. He was to teach them the language and literature of the Babylonians.

[5] The king assigned them a daily amount of food and wine from the king's table. They were to be trained for three years, and after that they were to enter the king's service.

[6] Among these were some from Judah: Daniel, Hananiah, Mishael and Azariah.

[7] The chief official gave them new names: to Daniel, the name Belteshazzar; to Hananiah, Shadrach; to Mishael, Meshach; and to Azariah, Abednego.

[8] But Daniel resolved not to defile himself with the royal food and wine, and he asked the chief official for permission not to defile himself this way.

[9] Now God had caused the official to show favor and sympathy to Daniel,

[10] but the official told Daniel, "I am afraid of my lord the king, who has assigned your food and drink. Why should he see you looking worse than the other young men your age? The king would then have my head because of you.

[11] Daniel then said to the guard whom the chief official had appointed over Daniel, Hananiah, Mishael and Azariah,

[12] "Please test your servants for ten days: Give us nothing but vegetables to eat and water to drink.

[13] Then compare our appearance with that of the young men who eat the royal food and treat your servants in accordance with what you see.

[14] So, he agreed to this and tested them for ten days.

[15] At the end of the ten days they looked healthier and better nourished than any of the young men who ate the royal food.

[16] So, the guard took away their choice food and the wine they were to drink and gave them vegetables instead.

The Mystery of Fasting

[17] To these four young men God gave knowledge and understanding of all kinds of literature and learning. And Daniel could understand visions and dreams of all kinds.
[18] At the end of the time set by the king to bring them in, the chief official presented them to Nebuchadnezzar.
[19] The king talked with them, and he found none equal to Daniel, Hananiah, Mishael and Azariah; so, they entered the king's service.
[20] In every matter of wisdom and understanding about which the king questioned them, he found them ten times better than all the magicians and enchanters in his whole kingdom.

This is a very important principle for us to see. Although Daniel and the three boys had the choice to eat food that was rich in substance and most likely tasted good to the flesh, they made the choice to eat only vegetables and water for ten days and then for three years continued this practice.

I'm certain the foods they could have eaten were meats, fats, pastries, and wine but verse 8 says, "Daniel resolved not to defile himself with the royal food and wine." Being Hebrew, there were foods that were forbidden in their own law and instead of making the law the culprit, they stated that a different diet would not make them any less than the others.

At the king's feast, there was quite possibly pork, shrimp, lobster, and other dainties that went against their consciences. As they stood for their principles and went with their Godly conviction, God granted them favor and a ten-day fast was extended for three years.

Resolving not to eat means Daniel made up his mind and that he determined beforehand not to eat certain foods. Our fast should be a predetermination to refrain from all foods. He rejected the rich foods that was his for the asking and most likely would have been supplied in abundance.

He and the three Hebrew boys became vegetarians for three years, living a consecrated life that consisted of water and vegetables. The New King James Version of Scripture translates the word vegetables in verse 12 with the word "pulse." Pulse consisted of vegetables, grains, wheat, barley, rye, peas, beans, and lentils. For three years, these same foods made up their diet. This diet was rich in protein and high in fiber.

However, God honored their commitment as verse 17 says, "As for these four young men, God gave them knowledge and skill in all literature and wisdom; and Daniel had understanding in all visions and dreams."

In verse 20, the Bible says, "And in all matters of wisdom and understanding about which the king examined them, he found them ten times better than all the magicians and astrologers who were in all his realm."

There was increased spiritual insight when it came to these men. In our generation, we try to fight witches; atheists and those of false religions in the flesh. We have debates and marches and seemingly make no real progress in the demise of these things that stand in opposition to the agenda of God in the earth. Often, we approach these things in our own strength and flesh by simply saying a prayer.

However, when we fast and God increases our knowledge and wisdom, there are things that those who are unbelievers cannot deny which becomes part of our lives.

The fact that you are smarter and wiser than others, who serve other gods, will set you apart. Remember, God is the One that promotes us—you are called to be obedient.

The more sensitive you become to the voice of the Holy Spirit, the more "seemingly intelligent you will become as your steps and your speech are now being directed by the Lord.

The Book of Daniel chapter 10 reveals that although Daniel did not fast, his consecration unto the Lord and his restricted diet was effective in releasing the answer that God desired.

The opposition was in the heavens as spiritual warfare took place between the angels of God and those of Satan.

Daniel 10:
[1] In the third year of Cyrus king of Persia, a revelation was given to Daniel (who was called Belteshazzar). Its message was true, and it concerned a great war. The understanding of the message came to him in a vision.
[2] At that time, I, Daniel, mourned for three weeks.

The Mystery of Fasting

[3] I ate no choice food; no meat or wine touched my lips; and I used no lotions at all until the three weeks were over.

[4] On the twenty-fourth day of the first month, as I was standing on the bank of the great river, the Tigris,

[5] I looked up and there before me was a man dressed in linen, with a belt of the finest gold around his waist.

[6] His body was like chrysolite, his face like lightning, his eyes like flaming torches, his arms and legs like the gleam of burnished bronze, and his voice like the sound of a multitude.

[7] I, Daniel, was the only one who saw the vision; the men with me did not see it, but such terror overwhelmed them that they fled and hid themselves.

[8] So, I was left alone, gazing at this great vision; I had no strength left, my face turned deathly pale and I was helpless.

[9] Then I heard him speaking, and as I listened to him, I fell into a deep sleep, my face to the ground.

[10] A hand touched me and set me trembling on my hands and knees.

[11] He said, "Daniel, you who are highly esteemed, consider carefully the words I am about to speak to you, and stand up, for I have now been sent to you. And when he said this to me, I stood up trembling.

[12] Then he continued, "Do not be afraid, Daniel. Since the first day that you set your mind to gain understanding and to humble yourself before your God, your words were heard, and I have come in response to them.

[13] But the prince of the Persian kingdom resisted me twenty-one days. Then Michael, one of the chief princes, came to help me, because I was detained there with the king of Persia.

[14] Now I have come to explain to you what will happen to your people in the future, for the vision concerns a time yet to come.

Daniel's consecration and his restricted diet consisted of no choice food or "pleasant bread" as the KJV translates verse 3. If defined, what this choice food meant was that, more than what he didn't eat, they are in reference to Daniel refraining from eating what he liked and what foods he did eat, he did not eat until he was full.

There was a spiritual breakthrough that Daniel desired and he knew that the only way he would experience God's victory was through his mourning and restricted diet. He didn't understand the reason for the dream he had and, further, didn't know why he didn't understand what it meant.

Remember, in chapter one, God gave him understanding in dreams and visions, yet this one vision remained elusive from his understanding. However, Daniel knew that the answer he sought would be found in God and he sought God out by consecrating.

There are times in our own lives when we will not eat our favorite foods for a period of time. Depending on the circumstance you face, there are times when nothing tastes good. You refrain from eating everything that brings you pleasure and, as a Christian, set aside time to seek God for His will in the situation.

Although the answer may not be as favorable as you feel it should be (as in the case of King David when he fasted for his son), you will be strengthened to accept God's plan for your life even if the outcome is not favorable.

David fasted for his son who was sick with hope that God would hear and allow him to live. However, his son was sick unto death and in the fast; David was strengthened to deal with the outcome which was that his son would die.

In our text here, it was twenty-one days before Daniel ate regular food. He was intent on receiving an answer from God.

Verse 8 says that he was weak from this fast and had no strength but was strengthened by the messenger from God (Gabriel) who had a fight with the prince of the Persian kingdom for three weeks.

This prince was not necessarily a person of royalty as much as he was a person of rank in this satanic empire. Although a powerful demon, he was not able to withstand the power of God in this situation and the same will be true in yours.

God will never let the prayers you offer while fasting to go unanswered. However, you must learn to put your flesh under subjection and stay on your knees until the answer manifests itself. If need be, God will send a reserve angel with your answer and make certain that you are not hurt in the midst of your fast.

The Mystery of Fasting

God answering your prayers by humbling yourself and praying is evident in the book of Ezra chapter 8. Here the people of God fasted for direction in their lives.

[21] There, by the Ahava Canal, I proclaimed a fast, so that we might humble ourselves before our God and ask him for a safe journey for us and our children, with all our possessions.

[22] I was ashamed to ask the king for soldiers and horsemen to protect us from enemies on the road, because we had told the king, "The gracious hand of our God is on everyone who looks to him, but his great anger is against all who forsake him.

[23] So, we fasted and petitioned our God about this, and he answered our prayer.

In verse 21, the KJV translates "a safe journey as *"to seek of Him a right way for us."* The people of God must see the importance of setting aside time before God before making some decisions for their lives and families.

As verse 23 says, *"they fasted and petitioned God and He answered their prayers."* Going without food without having a specific agenda before God is only going on another diet. It's a proven fact that most diets do not work.

You must combine your fast with prayers of petition before God. Petitioning God involves "Making a serious request; it's an appeal or plea to a superior from an inferior. It's also a formal written request made to an official person or organized body (as a court); a document embodying such a formal written request; something asked or requested."

The key is for you to be specific when you approach God. It's asking Him for something that you desire to see change in and that is the focal point for your prayers during the time you set aside to fast. Then God answers your prayers.

Then there are accounts in the Bible of people fasting or abstaining from all food. In second Chronicles chapter 20, King Jehoshaphat was in a great predicament. Warriors from three other kingdoms gathered to fight against him and he knew his army was not enough to stand against this magnitude of attack.

In our lives, there are times when we face certain dilemmas and don't know what to do. You don't have wisdom or resources to help you in your attack and you have prayed all you can pray.

Like the king here, it's time to proclaim a fast in your life that invokes the help of God in that situation.

When you do, strength and hope come that causes you to be firmly convinced that the battle you face is not something you have to do on your own as the battle will be in the hand of the Lord.

2 Chronicles 20 says:

[1] After this, the Moabites and Ammonites with some of the Meunites came to make war on Jehoshaphat.

[2] Some men came and told Jehoshaphat, "A vast army is coming against you from Edom, from the other side of the Sea. It is already in Hazazon Tamar (that is, En Gedi).

[3] Alarmed, Jehoshaphat resolved to inquire of the LORD, and he proclaimed a fast for all Judah.

[4] The people of Judah came together to seek help from the LORD; indeed, they came from every town in Judah to seek him.

[5] Then Jehoshaphat stood up in the assembly of Judah and Jerusalem at the temple of the LORD in the front of the new courtyard

[6] O LORD, God of our fathers, are you not the God who is in heaven?

You rule over all the kingdoms of the nations. Power and might are in your hand, and no one can withstand you.

[7] O our God, did you not drive out the inhabitants of this land before your people Israel and give it forever to the descendants of Abraham your friend?

[8] They have lived in it and have built in it a sanctuary for your Name, saying,

[9] If calamity comes upon us, whether the sword of judgment, or plague or famine, we will stand in your presence before this temple that bears your Name and will cry out to you in our distress, and you will hear us and save us.'

[10] But now here are men from Ammon, Moab and Mount Seir, whose territory you would not allow Israel to invade when they came from Egypt; so, they turned away from them and did not destroy them. [11] See how they are repaying us by coming to drive us out of the possession you gave us as an inheritance.

The Mystery of Fasting

[12] O our God, will you not judge them? For we have no power to face this vast army that is attacking us. We do not know what to do, but our eyes are upon you.

[13] All the men of Judah, with their wives and children and little ones, stood there before the LORD.

[14] Then the Spirit of the LORD came upon Jahaziel son of Zechariah, the son of Benaiah, the son of Jeiel, the son of Mattaniah, a Levite and descendant of Asaph, as he stood in the assembly.

[15] Listen, King Jehoshaphat and all who live in Judah and Jerusalem! This is what the LORD says to you: Do not be afraid or discouraged because of this vast army. For the battle is not yours, but God's.

There was a massive attack being waged against the people of God. There was no way they could win in the natural, therefore the king called a fast and received an answer from God.

What is awesome here is that they didn't put on a religious mask and begin making faith confessions about how they would win without seeking God first. The reality was they were going to lose without the Lord's intervention.

As you know we believe in speaking what God has spoken through our confession and we believe in extending faith in seemingly impossible situations. However, before you act you must know what the Spirit of God is declaring for that moment and that specific battle you face.

Demonic strongholds are allowed into our lives by acts of sin either by us or those are handed down from our forefathers, which we refer to as generational curses.

Your responsibility is to identify them, acknowledge that you have no power over them in your own strength, and then seek God declaring in the middle of your fast, "I have no power [in my own strength] to face this vast army that is attacking us. I do not know what to do, but my eyes are upon you."

If sin seems impossible and you find yourself constantly falling back into destructive behaviors, it's time for a fast to destroy those strongholds. These strongholds are things that come into your life to control you and keep you in bondage.

To be free from these things, you must first recognize these strongholds for what they are. Strongholds in its simplest defined manner are powerful ways in which demons have tried to control you.

2 Corinthians 4 gives a reference to strongholds and gives us wisdom in how to deal with them.

[3] For though we walk in the flesh, we do not war according to the flesh. [4] For the weapons of our warfare are not carnal but mighty in God for pulling down strongholds, [5] casting down arguments and every high thing that exalts itself against the knowledge of God, bringing every thought into captivity to the obedience of Christ, [6] and being ready to punish all disobedience when your obedience is fulfilled.

Defined, the Greek word for stronghold is **"ochÃroma"** and is fortification, a fortress used figuratively of any strong points or arguments in which one trusts. Therefore, you must be on guard for prior ways of thinking and erroneous teachings and principles from the world or even Bible teachers that are contrary to the Word of God.

They will set themselves up as strongholds, or impenetrable fortresses that are difficult to remove. However, this is where God has empowered us as His Church to destroy these fortresses through the Word of God and fasting. This combination of spiritual weaponry is an undefeatable force in the hand of a serious Christian. However, not everyone will experience this type of victory because not all Christians are willing to pay the price. It's much easier to wait on a prayer line and a bottle of anointing oil as a person who is known to have a healing ministry comes to town, so you can be relieved. Yet that's not God's intended plan. He wants you to learn to fight so you can still experience victory when the well-known preacher leaves town. Secondly, using Godly wisdom, you must disassociate yourself from people, places and things that link you to that stronghold. If you struggle with alcohol, remove yourself from people that drink and places where alcohol is served. The same is true with every other addiction. The irony is that, by choice, we become joined to people and things that God never intended. Then pay the price for years as you remain in bondage and destroy your life because you simply cannot get free. There was no covenant made between you and that person. You often don't want to hurt someone's feelings and, therefore, keep him or her around at the expense of hurting your own walk with God and, ultimately, God Himself. Thirdly, become skilled at speaking the Word of God over your life and refrain from speaking negatively about your situation. Don't give the devil glory and a further foothold in your life by saying how you'll never be free, how powerful he is, and how bad you have it. Ephesians 6:17 says, you must *"take the sword of the Spirit, which is the word of God." Taking this sword, you are first on the offensive and, being the Word of God, it goes beyond quoting the Scriptures.*

Literally, it is the "excellent use of the Word of God." This is applying it to your present situation in a manner as a skilled soldier. You must use God's appropriate scripture, speaking the Word of God in faith, believing that God has the power to do what He promised.

Your words must be full of faith declaring that God is in control of your life and is more powerful than the devil. Speak in agreement with God saying, If the Son sets me free, then I am free indeed! The Bible says the Word of God did not profit the children of Israel while they were in the desert because they did not mix it with faith. Let's not fall into that same trap, as faith must always be in operation in our lives. This is referred to as a living faith.

Nathaniel McNeil

4

FASTING – REVELATIONS FROM THE BIBLE

The Old Testament law specifically required fasting for only one occasion, which was the Day of Atonement. This Day of Atonement is immensely important. This day isn't a legal custom of the Jews or of Moses. Leviticus 23:1-3 reveals that God gives Moses His personal calendar of events when specific events would occur. Notice, the Bible says "these are the feast of the LORD" not of Moses or of the children of Israel but of the Lord. The word feast in Hebrew is "**moedim**," which means times or appointed times. So, when He says to Moses "these are the feasts of the LORD," He is saying these are the appointed times of the Lord. As you read, we will unfold these times to you. For example, is the Passover. Christ died exactly on the specific day of the Passover. Thus, Passover represented, as was practiced, a pointer to Jesus Christ as the sacrificial lamb. The feast of Firstfruit is exactly three days after Passover on which same Christ resurrects. Wow, mind blowing! "But every man in his own

The Mystery of Fasting

order: Christ the firstfruits; afterward they that are Christ's at his coming" (1 Corinthians 15:23).

"But now is Christ risen from the dead and become the firstfruits of them that slept" (1 Corinthians 15:20).

Here, Paul is referencing to the Feast of Firstfruits and thereby revealing that Christ is the fulfillment of it. How does all this point to fasting? It does since the Day of Atonement is the time of refreshing and cleansing and purification. In 2 Peter 3: 5-14, Peter speaks of this same cleansing of the earth as a prerequisite event in order to prepare it for the glory of God and the setup of a millennium period. So, this connects to fasting in the sense that during the time of atonements, the high priest must be sure all uncleanliness is away from him. Why? Because this is the time that the Shekinah, the very glory of God, would appear in the holy of holies in the temple. In other words, this cleansing and purification and preparation—which is a type of fasting—of the way for the glory to come down alludes to the fact that fasting is the preparation for the manifestation of the glory of God to be upon our lives.

This custom became known as "the day of fasting" (Jeremiah 36:6) or "the Fast" (Acts 27:9). MOST PEOPLE THINK Moses fasted during the forty days and forty nights he was on Mount Sinai receiving the law from God (Exodus 34:28). However, the Scripture does not indicate that Moses did a fast. Fasting is abstaining from food only not drink or water. So, what was Moses doing? Remember, this scripture says that Moses was in the presence of God. So, God sustained Moses to go forty days without water. Man can go extended periods without food but, without water, this is impossible without the help of God. Thus, because Moses was in the presence of God, he did not need to eat or drink. This does not constitute a biblical fast. King Jehoshaphat called for a fast in all Israel when they were about to be attacked by the Moabites and Ammonites (2 Chronicles 20:3). In response to Jonah's preaching, the men of Nineveh fasted and put on sackcloth (Jonah 3:5). Fasting was often done in times of distress or trouble. David fasted when he learned that Saul and Jonathan had been killed (2 Samuel 1:12). Nehemiah had a time of prayer and fasting upon learning that Jerusalem was still in ruins

(Nehemiah 1:4). Darius, the king of Persia, fasted all night after he was forced to put Daniel in the den of lions (Daniel 6:18). Fasting also occurs in the New Testament. Anna ***"worshipped night and day, fasting and praying"*** at the Temple (Luke 2:37). John the Baptist taught his disciples to fast (Mark 2:18). Jesus fasted for forty days and forty nights during which He was tempted by Satan (Matthew 4:2). The church of Antioch fasted (Acts 13:2) and sent Paul and Barnabas off on their first missionary journey (Acts 13:3). Paul and Barnabas spent time fasting for the appointment of elders in the churches (Acts 14:23).

The Mystery of Fasting

5

UNCOVERING THE BRIDEGROOM'S FAST

John the Baptist's disciples came to Jesus with a devoted and sincere question. They were confused and troubled by the lack of fasting among His disciples. John had taught his disciples to fast often, and they saw that even the hypocritical Pharisees recognized how essential the discipline was. Did Jesus not value fasting? Did He lack the discipleship and leadership skills to teach it to His men? John's disciples' intense hunger for God had led them to give up everything in their pursuit of Him. The implication behind their question was that John was a more spiritual leader than Jesus. Jesus answered their question by asking them what seemed a strange question. "Can the friends of the bridegroom mourn as long as the bridegroom is with them?" He then made another unusual statement saying, "the days were coming when the Bridegroom would be taken from them." He was referring to Himself as the Bridegroom who would be taken from them by dying on the cross. He implied that then His disciples would fast with the same consistency and intensity that John's disciples did. Their fasting, however, would flow out of longing and mourning for Jesus as a Bridegroom. Jesus used their question to introduce Himself as a Bridegroom. This was His first reference, in scripture, to being the Bridegroom. He was introducing a new paradigm of fasting—a fast motivated by the desire to encounter His beautiful and loving presence. In the Old Testament, fasting was usually an expression of sorrow over sin or a plea for God to physically deliver His people from disaster. In many cases, it had degenerated into a purely religious exercise, as the legalistic Pharisees practiced.

Now, the Lord was saying there was something new. After His death, after the New Covenant had been established, fasting would take on a whole new dimension. The indwelling Holy Spirit in each believer would make this possible. The fast His disciples would enter would be one related to intimacy with Jesus as the Bridegroom. In the New Covenant, God opened the depths of His heart to every believer through the Holy Spirit (1 Corinthians 2:10; Hebrews 10:19-22). It is a privilege beyond comprehension that weak humans can experience the depths of God's heart. This is our inheritance and our destiny. We must never be content to live without a growing experience of God's heart. *"For the Spirit searches all things, yes, the deep things of God ... We have received the Spirit that we might know the things freely given to us by God"* (1 Corinthians 2:10-12). The apostles experienced this intimacy of knowing the Man Christ Jesus while He walked the Earth. Jesus insisted that they not fast during this time but rejoice. Just as there will be no fasting in the age to come because we will be face to face with Him, it would have been unnecessary for the disciples to fast when God was their daily companion. But things changed for the apostles after Jesus was taken away by death. The promise of the New Covenant was still theirs— intimacy with Jesus—but His physical presence was gone. They mourned and longed to experience more of His presence. He had awakened a depth of desire in their hearts that they were not fully aware of until they were wounded by His absence. They longed for Him, for His nearness. When the overflowing gladness of His immediate presence was taken from them, they were heartsick. Then they fasted.

The Bridegroom Fast is About Desire
Song of Solomon 5:8 says, *"If you find my Beloved ... tell him I am lovesick!"* The Song of Solomon describes the relationship between Jesus, the Bridegroom, and the Church, His Bride. It represents the Church's lovesickness for God (Song 2:5; 5:8). Even the remembrance of our close encounters with Jesus in years passed creates a hunger today, a craving that will not be satisfied until we experience Him again and again in even greater measures. Lovesickness is mourning for the loving presence of Jesus as the Bridegroom God. No one can console our lovesick hearts except Him. A heart that does not mourn for more of Him is a heart that accepts its current state of spiritual barrenness as tolerable and livable. A mourning heart is fiercely discontent; it

has a desperate hunger for God. This is the Bridegroom Fast. The Bridegroom Fast is focused on desire: both understanding God's desire for us and awakening our desire for Him. God imparts new desires to us as He answers existent ones.

The hope of a lovesick heart will not be disappointed, for Jesus promised that we would be satisfied as we mourn for more of Him. "Blessed are those who mourn, for they shall be comforted" (Matthew 5:4). "Blessed are those who hunger and thirst for righteousness, for they shall be filled" (Matthew 5:6). The joy that the early apostles experienced in Jesus' nearness became grief and longing, even lovesickness when Jesus was taken from them.

These same longing and lovesickness have a dynamic purpose in us. Spiritual hunger is a divine gift that leads us to seek greater experiences of His love, regardless of the cost. It causes us to be willing to make whatever changes are necessary for our hearts and lives for love to have its way. We were made to love and be loved by God, and He has caused us to crave Him until our hearts' cry is answered. He increases our experience of Him by awakening and then answering desire within us.

First, in the initial stages, He romances us, lets us feel His love-stir within us. Though this brings a certain satisfaction to our souls, it also awakens a deeper longing and hunger for more. Once we taste just a little of God's presence, we cannot live without more of Him. This is the way God planned it. Hunger begets hunger and deep calls unto deep (Psalm 42:7). In every satisfaction God brings to us, we are left with an even greater desire for more of Him. It is by our hunger that He leads us into the fullness of love. We fast in response to the groan in our hearts for more of God.

The Purpose of the Bridegroom Fast
Why would Jesus want His friends to mourn while He was away? Isn't He a God of joy who wants His followers to live lives characterized by that same joy? These questions bring us to the heart of the Bridegroom Fast and its purpose. Yes, we were made to live in pleasure, but that joy can be found only in the person and presence of Jesus. Happiness apart from Jesus is no joy at all. Mourning and fasting for the Bridegroom is our way of positioning our hearts to live by the desire for God and not by the

The Mystery of Fasting

lusts of this age. Our mourning for Him gives witness that we are not of this world and that we refuse to come under the seductions of Satan, the ruler of this world. This holy longing will not ultimately or fully be satisfied until we live face to face with Jesus in the age to come.

His second coming is ultimately the fullness of the answer and consolation for which we mourn. It is in His coming that our highest joy will be found (Psalm 119:19,20; Romans 8:23-25; Hebrew 11:16). Until that day, however, we will continue to groan within ourselves, eagerly waiting for Him to come once again.

The purpose of the Bridegroom Fast goes even beyond yearning for Jesus' return—it is the yearning to experience His presence now. Amid the delay, the waiting between His first and second coming, God allows us to experience a measure of His presence. He has sent the Holy Spirit so we can encounter His presence and love in a measure even now. The Bridegroom Fast enlarges our hearts to experience that divine love and presence now.

God has designed us so that when we give ourselves to Him by fasting and praying the Word, our capacity to receive more of Him increases. No other dimension in the grace of God opens wide the deepest places of our beings like fasting and filling our hearts with the Scriptures that emphasize the truths of Jesus as our Bridegroom. Fasting catalyzes to increase the depth and the measure to which we receive from the Lord. By fasting, we receive greater measures of revelation at an accelerated pace, which has a deeper impact on our hearts.

One of the primary purposes of the Bridegroom Fast is to cause our hearts to move in love and longing for God. We do not fast to make God pay attention to us but to fully enter the affection and presence of God that is already ours in Christ. It is not to move His heart but to move our own. Our hearts are prone to dullness and lethargy, and if we don't deliberately confront that dullness, we become hardened without realizing it. The Bridegroom Fast tenderizes our hearts so dryness is diminished, and we can experience the affections of God in greater measure. Our hearts become tender, and our desire is nurtured as we experience the pleasures of knowing Him. I emphasize that our desire for God is His gift to us. However, this craving for God causes pain in our hearts. We are wounded in love. This works good things in us. He does not inflict meaningless heartache upon us, so we can be sure that this longing has a purpose. Spiritual hunger is a divine agent that leads us to greater love. It is an instrument that makes room for love and purity in our hearts and expands our souls.

We cannot enter the fullness of love without the preparatory impact of mourning for more of Him. Our desire for Jesus creates the grief or the pain of lovesickness, which in turn compels us to make changes in our lives so that we can receive all that is ours in God. We are wounded in love because He intentionally withholds a measure of His presence to bring us into greater intimacy as He works humility and produces meekness in us, so God's nearness is sustained in us for the long term. The Bridegroom Fast also brings holiness to our souls. Fasting for spiritual renewal includes mourning over the sin that hinders our relationship with Him.

The increase of lovesickness for God inevitably causes a conviction within, and we become unable to tolerate anything that opposes the life of God in us. No longer are we content to live in compromise or sin—we surrender everything because lovesickness compels us. Fasting is meant to "afflict" our souls as we renounce everything that sets itself up against the knowledge of God's love and power in our lives (Isaiah 58:3, 5). David spoke of humbling and chastening his soul with fasting as he confronted the sins that hindered his ability to behold the beauty of God (Psalm 27:4; 35:13; 69:10; 109:24). Fasting because of love exposes the compromises in our hearts and our ungodly dependence on worldly things. It is a way of keeping our hearts spiritually awake and alert in a dark world that naturally dulls and defiles the human spirit. Our love for God must be expressed in our quest to pursue total obedience.

Jesus said, "He who has My commandments and keeps them, it is he who loves Me. And he who loves Me will be loved by My Father, and I will love him and manifest Myself to him" (John 14:21). One key way to sustain our love in God as we seek to live righteously is to wage war with the lusts inside us. Lust has many different expressions, including pride, anger, covetousness, theft, immorality, pornography, bitterness, hatred, slander, jealousy, drunkenness, over-indulgence with food or entertainment, legal and illegal addictions, and others (Mark 7:21-22; Galatians 5:19-21; 1 John 2:16-17). 1 Peter 2:11 says, "Beloved, I beg you as sojourners and pilgrims, abstain from fleshly lusts which war against the soul."

So, mourning for the Bridegroom also involves repentance. To mourn is to rend or to tear our hearts, as the prophet Joel insisted: "Turn to Me with all your heart, with fasting, with weeping, and with mourning. So, rend your heart for He is gracious and merciful ..." (Joel 2:12-13). As we fast with hearts tender toward the Lord, we are kept in the position of continually rending our hearts and inviting the Holy Spirit to search us, to see if there is any wicked way in us (Psalm 139:23-24). Fasting is a God-given gift that helps us "break out" of the cares of this life and the corruption of sin and darkness. It enables us to get free from the grip of our culture's seductions that we might lay hold of the purpose for which God laid hold of us (Philippians 3:12).

A High Vision is Necessary for Fasting

Anyone who desires to live a life characterized by fasting must begin with a high vision, a vision to experience the fullness of what God wants to give each of us in this age. We fast because we cannot endure living in spiritual barrenness. The person who fasts understands the gap between what God wants to give them and what they are experiencing. The lack in our experience causes us to be discontent and to mourn. When we recognize that there is a realm in God to which we are invited but have not yet experienced, we become ruined. We must have this fullness. This state of "Guinness" is an essential part of the lifestyle of fasting. Without a vision or hope for attaining more in God, we will not fast. The Church today needs a renewed idea of fasting.

We need to recognize it as a gift from God that leads the human spirit into fascination and exhilaration before Him. God has given us the grace of the Bridegroom Fast that we might maximize the privilege of encountering the Bridegroom God, Jesus. Fasting is not intended by God to be something we hate. It is a gift meant to tenderize our hearts and bring a significant change in our lives. Fasting expresses our vision and determination to have more of God, and the pain of recognizing how we fall short. We fast because we believe God desires to take the vision, He has marked us with and bring it to fruition over time. We believe in Jesus' promise that there genuinely are rewards given by His Father, and we refuse to live as though these promises were not true (Matthew 6:17, 18).

New Wine and New Wineskins

"No one puts a piece of unshrunk cloth on an old garment; for the patch pulls away from the garment, and the tear is made worse. Nor do they put new wine into old wineskins, or else the wineskins break, the wine is spilled, and the wineskins are ruined. But they put new wine into new wineskins, and both are preserved" (Matthew 9:16-17).

Immediately after Jesus introduced the idea of the Bridegroom Fast, He spoke of new wine being placed into new wineskins (Matthew 9:16-17). It is notable that He prophesied of new wineskins in the context of the Bridegroom Fast. New wine speaks of the presence of the Holy Spirit and His impact on people as He releases the power in us that causes us to rejoice in love. His wine is always "new," for He continually imparts new and fresh revelation about God's heart. It is not that the Scriptures are new, but that the discovery of or emphasis on certain Scriptures is new to a particular generation. Right now, the Spirit is raising many men and women who are having and will have new and fresh encounters with Jesus.

They are the old treasures that the saints over the ages have experienced, yet, they are new to us. The result will be an anointed company of people who have fascinated and lovesick hearts for Jesus. But where does such a company of believers fit in with the current culture of spiritual compromise in the Church?

New Wineskins

New wineskins represent the new structures necessary to serve the people who have new wine experiences. The people of the new wine see God, themselves, and their missions very differently than they did before they encountered Jesus as the Bridegroom. They have new values and new paradigms of the Kingdom. These newly lovesick believers need new structures, and these new structures must be governed by leaders who share the benefits that flow from experiencing the Bridegroom's affections and power. Those with the old wineskin paradigms, values, and control cannot lead such people. Jesus spoke of new wineskins for that generation, pointing to the new structures that would come forth as a result of the outpouring of the Spirit on the day of Pentecost. He knew the synagogue system would not be enough to provide structure for those who were continually experiencing His power, revelation, and passion. Jesus was prophesying that the old structures would break, and the wine would spill out and be lost. The Lord soon replaced the existing old wineskin (the religious synagogue structure) with a New Testament community of believers led by unlikely people, such as fishermen, ex-prostitutes, and tax collectors. This principle of needing new wineskins for a new move of the Spirit has been repeated many times through history and will be repeated at the end of the age. Today, the Holy Spirit again desires to pour out new wine—the active presence of the Bridegroom. God will give us everything He provided the early Church. In the generation in which the Lord returns, the miracles of the Book of Acts will be combined with the wonders of the Book of Exodus. When the Holy Spirit comes in full manifest power, whatever wineskins do not agree with Him will be ruined and broken.

It's not possible to dwell with God except in unity with Him. The Holy Spirit's wine will only be continually poured out into an environment or structure that is suited to Him. The wine of the newly emphasized truths the Holy Spirit highlights in a revival is often lost in old systems. Nothing is more tragic than the wine being spilled and the Spirit's manifest presence and power left. Some old structures in this day will be revived and renewed. However, most will not. History shows that a new move of God is resisted by people. Significant changes are coming in our experiences, as well as with our Church and ministry structures. In the coming hour, untold millions will experience new dimensions of God's heart and power as they encounter Him as the Bridegroom King and Judge. The religious structures of today are predominantly led by those who are not lovesick. They will not know what to do with ex-prostitutes and fishers who are anointed with lovesickness. The Bridegroom Fast is one of the vehicles through which this wave of lovesickness will overtake the Church, resulting in the creation of new structures to accommodate them. The revelation of Jesus as the Bridegroom, along with the Bridegroom Fast, will be a vital part of transitioning from the old wineskin systems to New Testament Church structures and way of life.

The Mystery of Fasting

THE REWARDS OF FASTING

Then verse 8 begins the rewards of following God's kind of fast. It's not so much that your body will align itself with healing or your life with blessing. God gets involved with each area of your life.

"Then your light shall break forth like the morning, your healing shall spring forth speedily, and your righteousness shall go before you; the glory of the Lord shall be your rear guard."

Beginning with the word "then" God is saying, "At that time; soon after that; next in order of time; following next after in order of position.

Before you can experience this supernatural touch from heaven, you must first allow the first part of this chapter to be an important part of your life. When it is, you begin to experience a greater measure of "God's light, healing, righteousness, and a greater measure of God's glory.

If a person, a family, or a church experiences thing that are good, the first thing that you will find is God who is your rewarder. This will be evident as it is revealed to us as light.

Light makes vision possible, therefore you will see clearly what's ahead of you and will be led by God into His will for your life. You will know what you're supposed to do as God gives a greater understanding into His purposes for us.

The devil thought he could wipe you out, however, God has another plan. Because of your pain, hurt and everything that went wrong, you thought you would be buried alive. Yet you will recover your position of prominence as God determined.

Though grief tried to paralyze you, you will look as pleasant as the dawning of a new day. Those who are cheerful in doing good, God will make cheerful in enjoying good; and this also is a special gift from God. Those that have shown mercy shall find mercy.

The Mystery of Fasting

Secondly, your health shall spring forth speedily. Not only will your light break forth, but your health too, which is the healing of the wounds you have long complained of.

If you fast according to God's plan, your injustices shall be rectified, and you will renew your youth and recover thy vigor. Those that have helped others out of trouble will obtain help from God when it is their turn. God will put honor upon them. Good works shall be rewarded with a good name. This is included in that light which rises out of obscurity.

The Lord has promised us health through the suffering and sacrifice of the Lord Jesus. "He Himself bore our sicknesses and carried our sorrows, the chastisement of our peace was upon Him and by His stripes [wounds] we are healed.

Although you will not have to live a fasted life in order to get healed, and since your motives must remain pure, fasting has physical benefits that brings healing and blessing into your life. Literally, it deals with a restoration to soundness which, in addition to sound health, it also includes showing good judgment or sense. The people of God need wisdom, discretion and prudence. Fasting increases the capacity of your mind to receive direction from God for the decisions we make. It allows us the privilege to understand the times and know what we're supposed to do as in the case of the sons of Issachar and the consecration and restricted diet of Daniel, Shadrach, Meshach, and Abednego. If you need wisdom in any given situation, God releases what is desired and required through fasting.

Third, your righteousness shall go before you. God cares about how we live, act, and treat others. I often refer to acts of righteousness that is to reflect our position of righteousness we have when we became believers in Christ Jesus.

The reality is for most of us, our acts don't measure up to our position. Fasting God's way allows our acts to be more God-centered and focused. You find that it becomes easier to do what you know is right as you are now more sensitive to the Holy Spirit.

Your life takes a turn from giving in to every inclination of the flesh to having authority over it and making proper choices. Then, there's divine protection as verse 8 ends with saying that the glory of the Lord will be your rear guard or rereward as the KJV translates it. This is what the people in the book of Ezra experienced (Ezra 8:21.22).

God will lead you by His Word and give angels to protect you along the way. However, His glory will ensure that nothing sneaks upon you, taking you off guard. He wants to make certain that His people are divinely protected so they can accomplish the purpose for which they were born.

"Then you shall call, and the Lord will answer; You shall cry, and He will say, Here I am.' "If you take away the yoke from your midst, the pointing of the finger, and speaking wickedness." Verse 9 says the Lord will answer you *" if you will gain control of your actions by not being judgmental [or pointing the finger], removing the burdens that others find themselves under [removing the yoke of bondage] and taking control of your tongue by refusing to speak in a wicked manner."*

You must look at the good in all situations and consider how you say something while speaking things that will edify each other. Verse 12 says, *"Thou shalt be called (and it shall be to thy honor) the repairer of the breach, the breach made by the enemy in the wall of a city that was surrounded by the enemy."*

God wants to raise this generation of believers to make up the breach (or infringement against the commands of God) that has occurred in previous generations. Now grace is running out and the judgment of God is about to be released.

"Thou shalt be the restorer of paths, safe and quiet paths," not only to travel in, but to dwell in, so safe and quiet that people shall make no difficulty of building their houses by the road-side.

The fact is that, if you fast as God has chosen, He will settle them again in their former peace and prosperity, and there shall be none to make them afraid.

You are an important component to the greater purposes of God being done in the earth. You are going to be called a repairer of the break in the conscience of America and the other nations of the world as you obey this command.

Those from among you shall build the old waste places; you shall raise up the foundations of many generations; and you shall be called the Repairer of the Breach, The Restorer of Streets to Dwell

The Mystery of Fasting

In. Once these things are in place, verse fourteen becomes a reality for the Church of the Living God. It declares, "Then you shall delight yourself in the Lord; and I will cause you to ride on the high hills of the earth and feed you with the heritage of Jacob your father. The mouth of the Lord has spoken."

Psalm 37:4 says, *"Delight yourself in the Lord and He shall give you the desires of your heart."*

To delight yourselves in the Lord means to find pleasure in, enjoyment in Him, find your happiness in Him, and to find your joy in the Lord.

When you do, God will cause you to ride on the high hills of the earth and we'll be fed with the heritage of Jacob who is one of our patriarchal forefathers.

As I said, a heritage is an inheritance and looking at Jacobs's life, there was a tremendous promise made to him. This inheritance was not something that he accumulated during his lifetime but was something that he built upon—as did his father Isaac as he received it from Abraham.

This inheritance that Abraham received came as part of the fulfillment of the covenant God made with Him. The first part was that he would have descendants that would number as the stars in heaven and the sand on the seashore. Genesis chapter 15 says:

[1] After these things the word of the Lord came to Abram in a vision, saying, "Do not be afraid, Abram. I am your shield, your exceedingly great reward.

[2]   But Abram said, "Lord GOD, what will You give me, seeing I go childless, and the heir of my house is Eliezer of Damascus?

[3]   Then Abram said, "Look, You have given me no offspring; indeed, one born in my house is my heir!

[4]   And behold, the word of the Lord came to him, saying, "This one shall not be your heir, but one who will come from your own body shall be your *heir.*

[5]   Then He brought him outside and said, "Look now toward heaven, and count the stars if you are able to number them. And He said to him, "So shall your descendants be.

[6]   And he believed in the Lord, and He accounted it to him for righteousness.

[7]   Then He said to him, "I am the Lord, who brought you out of Ur of the Chaldeans, to give you this land to inherit it."

As Abraham was now coming near the end of his days, this promise of descendants would transcend the generation he lived in and include all the people who would call on the Name of the Lord through Jesus Christ.

We have all been added along with people from every land, tribe, tongue, and nation who call on the Name of the Lord, to be part of this great inheritance in order that this promise to Abraham would be fulfilled. This was not a natural promise but one that was spiritual and eternal in nature. This was the reinstitution of the eternal life that Adam forfeited in the Garden of Eden when he ate of the forbidden tree.

God knew that Abraham would obey him and therefore would be the man through whom the promised Messiah would come. God therefore grants eternal life, in addition to natural blessings while we go through this earth, to be our inheritance.

Genesis chapter 26 shows that the blessing of Abraham was inherited by his son Isaac and included increase from his labor and obedience.

Isaac knew that what you sowed you would reap, and he obeyed God in this command. He found that God was able to bless him and increase his harvest even during a drought and when men schemed to block his blessing by stopping up all his wells that were needed to water his crops.

"[12] Then Isaac sowed in that land and reaped in the same year a hundredfold; and the Lord blessed him. [13] The man began to prosper and continued prospering until he became very prosperous; [14] for he had possessions of flocks and possessions of herds and a great number of servants. So, the Philistines envied him. [15] Now the Philistines had stopped up all the wells which his father's servants had dug in the days of Abraham his father, and they had filled them with earth. [16] And Abimelech said to Isaac, "Go away from us, for you are much mightier than we."

Then in Genesis chapter 32, you have the heritage of Jacob including a change from a natural being to a spiritual being. This

The Mystery of Fasting

was evident in God changing his name from Jacob, meaning deceiver, to that of Israel meaning Prince of God.

Here, Jacob has an encounter with an angel, of whom some say was the Lord Jesus, and he fought him throughout the night. It's during this struggle that Jacob has a change in name which was an outward sign of the change in his nature. He was now positioned to be the person God wanted him to be.

"*[24] Then Jacob was left alone; and a Man wrestled with him until **the breaking of day.** [25] Now when He saw that He did not prevail against him, He touched the socket of his hip; and the socket of Jacob's hip was out of joint as He wrestled with him. [26] And He said, "Let Me go, for the day breaks. But he said, "I will not let You go unless You bless me! [27] So He said to him, "What is your name? He said, "Jacob. [28] And He*

said, "Your name shall no longer be called Jacob, but Israel; for you have struggled with God and with men and have prevailed. [29] Then Jacob asked, saying, "Tell me Your name, I pray. And He said, "Why is it that you ask about My name? And He blessed him there. [30] So Jacob called the name of the place Peniel: "For I have seen God face to face, and my life is preserved."

In Genesis 15:6, we read that "Abraham believed God and it was counted to him as righteousness. This was an Old Testament Saint living on New Testament grace. He looked forward to the cross and experienced the same grace you and I enjoy as we look back at the cross and walk in this earth without guilt and condemnation. Romans 4 gives us greater insight into this promise as we have the faith of Abraham extending and available to us all.

"[13] For the promise that he would be the heir of the world was not to Abraham or to his seed through the law, but through the righteousness of faith. [14] For if those who are of the law are heirs, faith is made void and the promise made of no effect, [15] because the law brings about wrath; for where there is no law there is no transgression. [

16] Therefore it is of faith that it might be according to grace, so that the promise might be sure to all the seed, not only to those who are of the law, but also to those who are of the faith of

Abraham, who is the father of us all [17] (as it is written, "I have made you a father of many nations) i€ in the presence of Him whom he believed" God, who gives life to the dead and calls those things which do not exist as though they did; [18] who, contrary to hope, in hope believed, so that he became the father of many nations, according to what was spoken, "So shall your descendants be. [19] And not being weak in faith, he did not consider his own body, already dead (since he was about a hundred years old), and the deadness of Sarah's womb. [20] He did not waver at the promise of God through unbelief, but was strengthened in faith, giving glory to God, [21] and being fully convinced that what He had promised He was also able to perform. [22] And therefore "it was accounted to him for righteousness." This is a huge promise as God desires for us to follow the faith that Abraham displays and therefore also become the recipients of the very same inheritance that he left for Isaac and Jacob.

Walking in this inheritance fulfills what the prophet Isaiah spoke in 58:14 which is natural and spiritual. However, it cannot be overemphasized that we must do so according to the example we have in the Word of God.

Part of our inheritance is the supernatural ability to walk in this type of faith. You're able to stand during your most severe trial and when all hope is gone, you'll still place your trust in God knowing that what God promised you, He is also able to perform. Just as natural as Jacob was renamed a spiritual Israel, you are now empowered to walk as a powerful spiritual being as part of your inheritance.

Knowing what's available and not applying the principles that God set up causes self-deception and we walk around trying to live a pipe dream, never living these things out as a reality in our lives.

However, this will not be so for those who walk in the inheritance of Jacob their father.

THE DEVIL IN THE BIBLE

The Mystery of Fasting

The Devil, also referred to as Satan, is best known as the nemesis of good people everywhere. His story has evolved over the years, but this malevolent being—and his legion of demons—continue to strike fear in people from all walks of life as the antithesis of all things good. Although the devil is present in some form in many religions and can be compared to some mythological gods, he's arguably best known for his role in Christianity. In modern biblical translations, the devil is the adversary of God and God's people.

It's commonly thought that the devil first showed up in the Bible in the book of Genesis as the serpent who convinced Eve—who then convinced Adam—to eat the forbidden fruit from the "tree of the knowledge" in the Garden of Eden. As the story goes, after Eve fell for the devil's conniving ways, she and Adam were banished from the Garden of Eden and doomed to mortality.

The devil was once the anointed cherub angel that covered the mercy seat and the throne of God. In the book of Isaiah and the fourteenth chapter, God is giving the prophet a dual revelation of the then literal king of Tyre but also of the invisible power in which he rules the kingdom. It reveals that though the man was the visible ruler, Satan himself was who gave this ruler his power. So, these verses are referencing both at the same time. Originally, Satan was the most beautiful living creature God created. In fact, no one could get, or approach God accept by him. He was the morning star and the anointed of God. Satan held the title of Lucifer who defied God and fell from grace. This revelation is based on the book of Isaiah in the Bible which says, "How art thou fallen from heaven, O Lucifer, son of the morning! How art thou cut down to the ground, which didst weaken the nations."

The book of Ezekiel includes another biblical passage which also points as a proof of the devil's existence. It admonishes the greedy king of Tyre but also refers to the king as a cherub who was once in the Garden of Eden. As a result, the king of Tyre was a personification of the devil.

The devil makes more appearances in the Bible, especially in the New Testament. Jesus and many of his apostles warned people to stay alert for the devil's cunning enticements that would lead them to ruin. And it was the devil who tempted Jesus in the wilderness to "fall down and worship him" in exchange for riches and glory.

HOW DEMONS MISLEAD
To mislead people, demons use Spiritism. The practice of Spiritism is involvement with demons, both in a direct way and through a human medium. The Bible condemns Spiritism and warns us to keep free from everything connected with it (Galatians 5:19-21). Spiritism does for the demons what bait does for fishermen. A fisherman uses a variety of baits to catch various kinds of fish. Similarly, wicked spirits use different forms of Spiritism to bring all sorts of people under their influence.

One type of bait used by the demons is divination. What is divination? It is an attempt to find out about the future or about something unknown. Some forms of divination are astrology, the use of tarot cards, crystal gazing, palmistry, and the search for mysterious omens, or signs, in dreams. Although many people think that practicing divination is harmless, the Bible shows that fortune-tellers and wicked spirits work together. For instance, Acts 16:16-18 mentions "a demon of divination" that enabled a girl to practice fortune-telling. But she lost this ability when the demon was cast out of her.

Another way that demons mislead people is by encouraging them to inquire of the dead. People grieving over the death of a loved one are often deceived by wrong ideas about those who have died. A spirit medium may give special information or may speak in a voice that seems to be that of a dead person. As a result, many people become convinced that the dead are alive and that contacting them will help the living to endure their grief. But any such "comfort" is false as well as dangerous. Why? Because the demons can imitate the voice of a dead person and give a spirit medium information about the one who died (1 Samuel 28:3-19). Moreover, as we learned in Chapter 6, the dead have ceased to exist (Psalm 115:17). So "anyone who inquires of the dead" has been misled by wicked spirits and is acting contrary to the will of God (Read: Deuteronomy 18:10, 11; Isaiah 8:19). Therefore, be careful to reject this dangerous bait used by demons.

Wicked spirits not only mislead people, but they also frighten them. Today, Satan and his demons know that they have only "a short period of time" left before they are put out of action, and they are now more vicious than ever (Revelation 12:12, 17). Even so, thousands of people who once lived in daily dread of such wicked spirits have been able to break free. How did they do this? What can a person do even if he is already involved in Spiritism? This question will lead us to the next point of discussion.

FASTING: KEY TO BREAKTHROUGH!

The Bible tells us both how to resist wicked spirits and how to break free from them. Consider the example of the first century Christians in the city of Ephesus. Some of them practiced Spiritism before becoming Christians. When they decided to break free from Spiritism, what did they do? The Bible says: ***"Quite a number of those who practiced magical arts brought their books together and burned them up before everybody"*** (Acts 19:19). By destroying their books on magic, those new Christians set an example for those who wish to resist wicked spirits today. People who want their fasting to be accepted must get rid of everything related to Spiritism. That includes books, magazines, movies, posters, and music recordings that encourage the practice of Spiritism and make it seem appealing and exciting. Included, too, are amulets or other items worn for protection against evil (1 Corinthians 10:21). Some years after the Christians in Ephesus destroyed their books on magic, the apostle Paul wrote them:

"We have a struggle ... against the wicked spirit forces" (Ephesians 6:12). The demons had not given up. They were still trying to gain an advantage. So, what else did those Christians need to do? ***"Besides all of this,"*** said Paul, ***"take up the large shield of faith, with which you will be able to extinguish the entire wicked one's [Satan's] burning arrows"*** (Ephesians 6:16). The stronger our shield of faith, the greater our resistance to wicked spirit forces will be (Matthew 17:20). How, then, can we strengthen our faith? By studying the Bible. The firmness of a wall depends very much on the strength of its foundation. In the same way, the firmness of our faith depends greatly on the strength of its base, which is accurate knowledge of God's Word, the Bible. If we read and study the Bible daily, our faith will become strong. Like a strong wall, such faith will shield us from the influence of wicked spirits (1 John 5:5). What other step did those Christians in Ephesus need to take? They needed further protection because they were living in a city filled with demonism. So, Paul told them: ***"With every form of prayer and supplication . . . carry on fasting and prayer on every occasion in spirit"*** (Ephesians 6:18). Since we too live in a world full of demonism, earnestly praying to God for his protection is essential in resisting wicked spirits. Of course, we need to use God's name in our prayers (Read: Proverbs 18:10). Hence, we should keep on praying to God: ***"Deliver us from the wicked one,"*** Satan the devil (Matthew 6:13). God will answer such earnest prayers (Psalm 145:19). Wicked spirits are dangerous, but we need not live in fear of them if we oppose the devil and draw close to God by doing His will (Read: James 4:7, 8.) The power of wicked spirits is limited. They were punished in Noah's day, and they face their final judgment in the future (Jude 6). Remember, too, that we have the protection of God's powerful angels (2 Kings 6:15-17). Those angels are deeply interested in seeing us succeed in resisting wicked spirits. The righteous angels are cheering us on, so to speak. Let us therefore stay close to Jehovah and his family of faithful spirit creatures. May we also avoid every kind of Spiritism and always apply the counsel of God's Word (1 Peter 5:6, 7; 2 Peter 2:9). Then we can be sure of victory in our fight against wicked spirit creatures.

Jesus makes a bold promise to His followers in Matthew 6:17-18 (Endorsed by the Holy Spirit, no less, because He oversaw WHAT got published in God's Word, so two-thirds of the Godhead are in complete agreement on the matter, for any skeptics!): That if they will fast by the inner prompting of the Holy Spirit and just because of wisdom, they will be given a reward from the Father. I can personally attest to the fact that every time I have fasted, God has rewarded me in one way or another. Often the rewards come after I've stopped fasting. No—I didn't always receive from Him everything I would like to have received from Him in my fasting—but He let me KNOW He was pleased with my fasting

The Mystery of Fasting

by a reward of some sort that I KNOW I would not have received from Him otherwise. So, in conclusion, it is my own experience that one can never come up short fasting. When their primary reason is to either have sinful/harmful strongholds—demonic assignments—broken, in need of healing, see miraculous provision provided in times of great need, and/or to try to gain greater intimacy with God which is what I believe should always be the primary reason to fast in the first place.

HUNGER AND THIRSTING
"Blessed are those who hunger and thirst for righteousness, for they shall be satisfied" (Matthew 5:6).
"Blessed are those who hunger and thirst for righteousness."
We hear those words on the lips of Jesus in the Sermon on the Mount. But, too often we misunderstand what He's saying. Some thought that people who hunger and thirst for righteousness are those who are so zealous to do good deeds that they are constantly gobbling up righteousness at every turn. They sort of sounded like a religious Pac-Man—a compulsive eater of good deeds. Their imagination always concocted a picture of a Mother Teresa type person—someone who had an insatiable appetite for goodness that sent them on a 24/7 quest for pious accomplishments.

There's a problem with that interpretation: it completely misses what it means to hunger and thirst. Hungering and thirsting are a recognition of our emptiness. I only hunger when I recognize that my belly is empty. I only thirst when I know that I'm parched. Hungering and thirsting are a groaning acknowledgment that I'm lacking something that I desperately need—food and drink. So, when you hunger and thirst for righteousness, you're recognizing that you don't have any. Hunger and thirst are our body's alarm system. There's something akin to panic in hungering and thirsting. Like a dinging "low fuel" light on your dashboard. Jesus is saying that people who realize that their righteousness tank is damnably empty will be "satisfied". How is that? Is it because they're going to finally learn how to get their act together? Are we lawbreakers going to finally start pulling our weight and earning our keep? Paul says that never happens. In

Romans 3, he explains: "For by works of the law no human being will be justified in his sight."

So, how's it going to happen? How are those who see their bankruptcy going to be satisfied? Romans 3:21 explains it: ***"But now, apart from the law, the righteousness of God has been revealed, attested by the Law and the Prophets."***

Isn't that amazing? The righteousness of God that has been revealed is none other than Christ Himself. He's our righteousness. He's the satisfaction for people who hunger and thirst.

All too often when we come to the Lord's table, we try to reflect on how well we've done lately with our righteous deeds. We're guilty of coming to the table forgetting that we're truly hungry. But, that's precisely when we need to remember our hungering and thirsting. The Lord's table is that satisfaction that Jesus spoke of in the Sermon on the Mount. In John 6, He says that His body and blood are precisely the life-giving food and drink that we so urgently need. *"Truly, truly, I say to you, unless you eat the flesh of the Son of Man and drink his blood, you have no life in you. Whoever feeds on my flesh and drinks my blood has eternal life, and I will raise him up on the last day. For my flesh is true food, and my blood is true drink. Whoever feeds on my flesh and drinks my blood abides in me, and I in him. As the living Father sent me, and I live because of the Father, so whoever feeds on me, he also will live because of me. This is the bread that came down from heaven, not like the bread the fathers ate, and died. Whoever feeds on this bread will live forever."*

BREAKING SATAN'S STRONGHOLDS IN YOUR LIFE

Ephesians 4:27, 30

I know there are many Christians who have an evil stronghold in their life. It's harming them, wrecking their spiritual life, contaminating the life of their family and church. The devil has found an unclean place within and built a foul nest, a beachhead, a

The Mystery of Fasting

stronghold there. And he uses that stronghold to war against God and His work.

"For a great door and effectual is opened unto me, and there are many adversaries." Adversities—Greek is **antikeimai** which means to lie opposite and withstand. Some forces oppose and face your actions to advance. So, for every move you make toward great things in your life, there are enemies in the spirit realm you cannot see that are opposing it. Therefore, families shatter, relationships break down, the reason for no healing, emotional distress of every kind.

Ephesians 4 says, [27] ***Neither give place to the devil verse [30] and grieve not the Holy Spirit of God.*** We should sit up and take notice: on the one hand, we could give place to the devil and on the other grieve the Holy Spirit. Either one should be unthinkable. What does it mean to "give place to the devil"? Let's say you own 50 acres of land, and I want one acre right in the middle of it. You sell it to me. Now, I have the right to go onto your property at will, to get to my one acre. I start throwing trash around and playing loud music all hours of the night. I'm desecrating your property, but there's nothing you can do—you've given me access. You try to make me leave, and I say, "I'm not going, and you can't make me go. I have a legal right to it. If you don't like it---too bad!" You wouldn't be able to move me out because you gave me a place there.

Some of you have done the same thing for Satan! You cannot dislodge him unless you remove him legally because you have given him a place. He owns some strongholds in your life.

"And be renewed in the spirit of your mind; And that ye put on the new man, which after God is created in righteousness and true holiness." It's not enough to put off the old man; you must put on the new man. "And be not drunk with wine wherein is excess but be filled with the Spirit" (Ephesians 5:18).

To be "filled with the Spirit" means there's not one room in your temple where God is shut out, not one closet that He doesn't have a key. In your romantic life, family life, business life, political life, church life, social life—in your money, your exercise, your sleep, your eating, "in my lying down, in my waking up, Jesus, I give you the keys to it all." [30] And grieve not the Holy Spirit of God, whereby ye are sealed unto the day of redemption.

You have a choice; you can grieve the Spirit of God and be filled with the devil, or you can put the devil out and be filled with the Spirit of

God. You're never going to cease grieving the Holy Spirit; you're never going to erase Satan from your life until you choose against Satan and yield to God's Holy Spirit.

"Howbeit this kind go out except by prayer and fasting" **Matthew 17:21.**

Choose This Fast

"Is this not the fast that I have chosen: To lose the bonds of wickedness, To undo the heavy burdens, To let the oppressed go free, And that you break every yoke?" (Isaiah 58:6).

The proper fast will break all strongholds on your life! Fasting deals not with water but food. Fasting is to abstain from eating voluntarily. Fasting was not used as punishment but as an instrument and blessing of power. This is a real fast, to abstain from food. Not water but food! Many have thought they were fasting and had not received the blessings of every yoke broken because they have fasted without full knowledge of what fasting is and how to do it. Let's speak of the Daniel Fast. Is there such a thing as the Daniel Fast?

The Scripture says that Daniel **mourned** *not fasted*; we must not confuse fasting with mourning. Although, there is mourning in fasting.

"In the third year of Cyrus King of Persia a thing was revealed unto Daniel, whose name was called Belteshazzar; and the thing was true, but the time appointed was long: and he understood the thing and had an understanding of the vision. In those days, I Daniel was mourning three full weeks. I ate no pleasant bread, neither came flesh nor wine in my mouth, neither did I anoint myself at all, till three whole weeks were fulfilled" (Daniel 10:1-3).

Mourning pronounced means to be languid or walk with head cast down. The root of this word implies the sense of falling which is

The Mystery of Fasting

done by mourners. Daniel was unwilling to enjoy or exact pleasures until he got some answers.

Rather than enjoy pleasantries, he desired revelation of what would befall his people. He avoided what was not necessary or essential for a season to seek God. When mourning, you lack the desire for things because you miss something else. Here, Daniel is acting as though a death had occurred and revealed his great desire for the spiritual. Daniel mourned, meaning he had an outward action of his grief for his people and the revelation of their end. He was expressing sorrow and anguish outwardly which he had inwardly for revelation.

"The LORD is nigh unto them that are of a broken heart; and saveth such as for being of a contrite spirit" (Psalm 34:18).

What fast have you chosen? Most of us would probably answer that question with a list of what we're eating, what we're not eating, and for how long. It's all too easy to become so focused on what we're giving up that we lose sight of what's to gain.

God answered that question in Isaiah 58. He has chosen a fast that loosens bonds of wickedness, lifts heavy burdens, frees those who are oppressed and breaks every yoke. When you grab hold of this truth— the fast God has chosen—your focus can shift from the sacrifices you're making to the promises you're waiting.

Is there something in your life that has you bound, weighed down, and held back from your destiny? Are you "yoked" to a bad habit, an iniquity, a habitual sin? Do you live with the weight of regret, depression, or discouragement, with the burden of providing for your family in a shaky economy with the pressure of children, a spouse, or parents who are not saved?

As you fast, cry out to the Lord to break those bonds, lift those burdens that make you feel hopeless and helpless. Let Him put the pieces back together in your own life, then He can empower you to rescue others, to feed the hungry, to house the poor and the outcasts, and to clothe the naked. And what does God say will come next:

"Then your light shall break forth like the morning,
Your healing shall spring forth
speedily, And your righteousness shall
go before you;

*The glory of the LORD shall be your rear guard.
Then you shall call, and the Lord will
answer; You shall cry, and He will say,
'Here I am.'"* (Isaiah 58:8-9).

So again, I ask, "What fast have you chosen?" What is the Holy Spirit whispering to your heart? Is there something you need to let go? Or maybe something it's time to get? This is the fast you have chosen. Remember it. Put it in front of you. And remember— when you are weak, He is strong.

"The sacrifices of God are a broken spirit: a broken and a contrite heart, O God, thou wilt not despise" (Psalm 51:17).

"For thus saith the high and lofty One that inhabiteth eternity, whose name is Holy; I dwell in the high and holy place, with him also that is of a contrite and humble spirit, to revive the spirit of the humble, and to revive the heart of the contrite ones" (Isaiah 57:15).

"For all those things hath my hand made, and all those things have been, saith the LORD: but to this man will I look, even to him that is poor and of a contrite spirit, and trembleth at my word" (Isaiah 66:2).

God is looking for some people to whom nothing else matters but God. Satan wants to use your breaking points. Being broken shuts the door on your breaking points. We must be inspired by God on when to fast and how to fast to access the wonders from God. Our fast becomes most potent when we fast with this attitude and commitment.

FASTING: A WEAPON THAT BRINGS HEALING, DELIVERANCE AND BREAKTHROUGHS

Strongholds of drugs, and other addictions must go when we pray with fasting.

"he giveth power to the faint; and to them that have no might he increaseth strength.

The Mystery of Fasting

[30] even the youths shall faint and be weary, and the young men shall utterly fall:
[31] But they that wait upon the lord shall renew their strength; they shall mount up with wings as eagles; they shall run, and not be weary; and they shall walk, and not faint" (Isaiah 40:29).
Wait in verse 31 is **qavah**, in Hebrew, means to twist and to bind a rope, to be strong, strengthen, expect, and look eagerly.
So, this waiting is waiting of building strength, twist the rope to make it stronger, waiting, expect, upon the lord. How? By doing what he tells us to do in order to build and strengthen ourselves. We will be built up to soar as eagles.
Fasting is the type of waiting that builds us and renews strength. Fasting is how we build power before we are attacked. We can soar as eagles.
"if thou faint in the day of adversity, thy strength is small" (Proverbs 24:10). When we resort to our flesh to handle and deal with adversity, we have fainted and have small strength. This scripture reveals we must have power reserved for the day we need it.
"howbeit this kind goeth not out but by prayer and fasting" (Matthew 17:21).
Demons don't respond to wishes and just desires. They respond to power. Many forget this here.
Exousia is authority
Dunamis is dynamic, revealed, manifested power.
Now you may have authority to do something but lack the power or energy to do it.
This scripture reveals why Jesus fasted because though he had authority to cast out demons, he needed also the dunamis, the manifested power.
Our word must come from our spirits. If our spirits are strong, the devil must answer. But if weak, he will ignore us.
Fasting isn't done to be seen in the sense of being lifted up. Moreover, when ye fast, be not, as the hypocrites, of a sad countenance: for they disfigure their faces, that they may appear unto men to fast. Verily I say unto you, they have their reward" (Matthew 6:16).

Their reward is to be noticed of men. They have no spiritual connection to their fasting at all. It's done from the flesh.

Therefore, they had no spiritual power, from God. And those who had spiritual power, were sorcerers who used mediums. They had no power because they lacked the proper motives for fasting.

When the church has lost its true mission and purpose, when the kingdom of God is not sought at any cost with fasting and strong prayers, you are left with pretense and material things as the value of ministry and life.

They valued fame, fortune, and prestige above true sheer dynamic power with God.

"but thou, when thou fastest, anoint thine head, and wash thy face; That thou appear not unto men to fast, but unto thy father which is in secret: and thy father, which seeth in secret, shall reward thee openly" (Matthew 6:17-18).

In secret here is the Greek word *kryptos*—which means hidden, concealed, that which is not seen.

Now Jesus could not have meant that no one is to know your fasting, because national fasts were still prevalent in his day.

So, what does he mean when he uses the Greek word kryptos? He speaks of the hidden part of man which is his spirit. We are to fast from our spirits. See, Jesus was led by his spirit into the wilderness to fast.

A true fast will emanate from our spirit, a cry for true power and nearness to God. This is the secret place of our spirits.

Our spirits originated this fast not our flesh and for carnal reasons. When our spirits drive us into fasting, it is a secret fast that God honors with the right motives.

Then he will reward us. Reward—Greek **apodidomi**—means obligated to render what is due.

When we fast with the right spirit, then God is obligated to render what is due. He is obligated to deliver, heal, set free, send breakthrough. But this word also means with swiftness, speed and far more exceedingly than what is due.

God doesn't accept a fast full of pride and the flesh but one from the spirit of man.

"bring forth therefore fruits meet for repentance:" (Matthew 3:8).

"for whosoever exalteth himself shall be abased; and he that humbleth himself shall be exalted" (Luke 14:11).

Fasting is humbling ourselves before God that he might exalt us. Our fast, as our prayers, must come from the secret place—our spirits. Thus, a fast is connecting your physical body to the spirit or spiritualizing your body.

Your body becomes the point of contact for the power and glory and the presence of God.

Fasting speeds up the process of manifested prayers and healing. Isaiah 58: 8 tells us that our healing will spring forth speedily and the glory of God shall be our real, true experience.

Healing of all types—if something is not well emotional sickens, physical sickness, mental sickness—fasting will heal and not just heal but do it speedily.

I am not a medical doctor, nor do I claim to be one. I am just revealing what the scriptures say concerning these matters.

If you desire to be healed even from a bad relationship, fasting will bring healing. And the glory of God manifested in your life. When we fast, we provoke speedy recovery and restoration. No matter what it is.

The book of Esther 5:1-23 tells us how a nation's story changed from death to life through the mystery of fasting. God turned the captivity and restored normalcy.

God caused the man who desired to destroy a nation of people to be reversed speedily and changed the story of a cup bearer to a leader in the kingdom all from one fast and it happened with quickness.

Matthew 10:1 states all manner of sickness was healed.

I prophesy that as you practice fasting, your situation will be turned around speedily.

FASTING: A KEY TO STRONG FAITH

Nathaniel McNeil

Faith is the rule to access experience and the more profound things of God. Also, you need faith for promotion to higher levels of power in God where yokes are destroyed, and your hardest prayers are manifested. Fasting is the spiritual price paid through hunger. The price for power isn't money, but it does have value. The price is fasting. *"Then came the disciples to Jesus apart, and said, Why could not we cast him out? And Jesus said unto them, Because of your unbelief; for verily I say unto you, If ye have faith as a grain of mustard seed...nothing shall be impossible to you. Howbeit, this kind goeth not out but by prayer and fasting"* (Matthew 17:19-21).

When the disciples saw Jesus cast the evil spirit out of the person with epilepsy whom "they could not cure," they asked the Master for the cause of their failure. He had given them "power and authority over all Devils, and to cure all diseases" (Luke 9:1). They had often exercised that power and joyfully told how the devils were subject to them. And yet now, while He was on the Mount, they had utterly failed. There had been nothing in the will of God or about the case to render deliverance impossible—that had been proved. At Christ's bidding, the evil spirit had gone out. From their expression, "Why could we not?" it is evident that they had wished and sought to do so. They had probably used the Master's name and called upon the evil spirit to go out. Their efforts had been vain, and, in the presence of the multitude, they had been put to shame. "Why could we not?"

Christ's answer was direct and understandable: *"Because of your unbelief."* The cause of His success and their failure was not owing to His having a special power to which they had no access. No, the reason was not far to seek. He had so often taught them that there is one power, that of faith, to which, in the kingdom of darkness, as in the kingdom of God, everything must bow. In the spiritual world, failure has but one cause, the want of faith. Faith is the one condition on which all divine power can enter man and work through him. It is the susceptibility of the unseen: man's will yielded up to and molded by the will of God. The power they had received to cast out devils, they did not hold in themselves as a permanent gift or possession. The power was in Christ, to be received, and held, and used by faith alone, living faith in Himself. Had they been full of faith in Him as Lord and Conqueror in the spirit world, had they been full of faith in Him as having given the authority to cast out in His name, this faith would have given them the victory. ***"Because of your unbelief"*** was, for all time, the Master's explanation and reproof of impotence and failure in His church.

Strong Faith

But such want of faith may have a cause too. Well, might the disciples have asked: "And why could we not believe? Our faith has cast out devils before this: why have we now failed in believing?" The Master proceeds to tell them ere they ask: "This kind goeth not out but by prayer and fasting." As faith is the simplest, so it is the highest exercise of the spiritual life, where our spirit yields itself in perfect receptivity to God's Spirit, and so is strengthened to its highest activity. This faith depends entirely upon the state of the spiritual life; only when this is strong and in full health when the Spirit of God has full sway in our life, that's where the power of faith does its mighty deeds.

Therefore, Jesus adds: "Howbeit this kind goeth not out but by prayer and fasting." The faith that can overcome such stubborn resistance as you have just seen in this evil spirit, Jesus tells them, is not possible except to men living in very close fellowship with God, and in exceptional separation from the world in prayer and fasting. And so, He teaches us two lessons regarding the worship of profound importance: The one, that faith needs a life of worship in which to grow and keep strong. The other, that prayer requires fasting for its full and perfect development.

Faith Needs a Life of Prayer

Faith is the truth and revelation which is the divine word. Faith needs a life of prayer for its full growth. In all the different parts of the spiritual life, there is such close union, such unceasing action, and reaction, that each may be both cause and effect. Thus, it is with faith. There can be no real prayer without faith; some

measure of faith must precede prayer. And yet prayer is also the way to more faith. There can be no higher degree of faith except through much prayer. This is the lesson Jesus teaches here.
There is nothing needed so much to grow as our faith. "Your faith groweth exceedingly," is said of one church (2 Thessalonians 1:3). When Jesus spoke the words, "according to your faith be it unto you" (Matthew 9:29), He announced the law of the kingdom, which tells us that all have not equal degrees of faith, that the same person has not always the same degree, and that the measure of faith must still determine the measure of power and blessing. If we want to know where and how our faith is to grow, the Master points us to the throne of God. It is in prayer, in the exercise of the faith I have, in fellowship with the living God, that faith can increase. Faith can only live by feeding on what is divine, on God Himself.
It is in the adoring worship of God, the waiting on Him and for Him, the deep silence of the soul that yields itself for God to reveal Himself, that the capacity for knowing and trusting God will be developed. It is as we take His word from the Blessed Book, and bring it to Himself, asking Him to speak it to us with His living, loving voice, that the power will come fully to believe and receive the word as God's word to us. It is in prayer, in living contact with God in living faith, that faith—the power to trust God, and in that trust, to accept everything He says, to accept every possibility He has offered to our faith—will become strong in us. Many Christians cannot understand what is meant by the much prayer they sometimes hear spoken. They can form no conception, nor do they feel the need for spending **hours** with God. But what the Master says, the experience of His people has confirmed: men of strong faith are men of much prayer.
Jesus, before telling us to believe that we receive what we ask, first said, ***"Have faith in God"*** (Mark 11:22). It is God, the living God, into whom our faith must strike its roots deep and broad. Then it will be strong to remove mountains and cast out devils.
"And Jesus said unto them, Because of your unbelief: for verily I say unto you, If ye have faith as a grain of mustard seed, ye shall say unto this mountain, Remove hence to yonder place, and

it shall remove, and nothing shall be impossible unto you" (Matthew 17:20).

Oh! If we do but give ourselves up to this work God has for us in the world, coming into contact with the mountains and the devils there are to be cast away and cast out, we should soon comprehend the need there is of much faith, and of much prayer. This is as the soil in which alone faith can be cultivated.

Christ Jesus is our life, the life of our faith too. It is His life in us that makes us strong and makes us simple to believe. It is in the dying to self which much prayer implies, in closer union to Jesus, that the spirit of faith will come in power. Faith needs prayer for its full growth.

PREPARATION FOR MINISTRY

Fasting delivers you from the actions and manifestation of the flesh in your life in order for you to walk in the ways of God. *"watch and pray, that ye enter not into temptation: the spirit indeed is willing, but the flesh is weak"* (Matthew 26:41).

The flesh is weak. As we weaken the flesh in fasting, we make greater the power and energy of the spirit within us.

Our spirit is willing, but we make it strong and full of power to lead our flesh man and subdue it.

This is done through the mystery of fasting. *"it is the spirit that quickeneth; the flesh profiteth nothing: the words that I speak unto you, they are spirit, and they are life"* (John 6:63). The spirit quickeneth unto righteous living. This flesh must be subdued to do the will of God. We are commanded to walk in the spirit. *"Verily, verily, I say unto you, except a corn of wheat fall into the ground and die, it abideth alone: but if it dies, it bringeth forth much fruit"* (John 12:24).

It is the sacrifice of fasting that God views and empowers us to overcome the flesh and render it dead that our spirit us in all things. Many attempts to deliver themselves by them attempting to subdue the flesh. When I say we are to subdue the flesh I mean that we through our spirit subdue the flesh. There is a big difference.

There is therefore now no condemnation to them which are in Christ Jesus, who walk not after the flesh, but after the spirit. For the law of the spirit of life in Christ Jesus hath made me free from the law of sin and death" (romans 8:1-2).

When we walk according to the spirit, we will not fulfill the lust of the flesh.

When we fast in from our spirit man, we subdue the flesh

"***[13] for if ye live after the flesh, ye shall die: but if ye through the spirit do mortify the deeds of the body, ye shall live. For as many as are led by the spirit of God, they are the sons of God"*** (romans 8:13-14).

Jesus was led of the spirit to fast.

We must fast in the spirit and of the spirit to subdue the flesh. It's a sacrifice unto the lord.

[25] because the foolishness of God is wiser than men; and the weakness of God is stronger than men.

[26] For ye see your calling, brethren, how that not many wise men after the flesh, not many mighty, not many noble, are called:

[27] But God hath chosen the foolish things of the world to confound the wise; and God hath chosen the weak things of the world to confound the things which are mighty;

[28] And base things of the world, and things which are despised, hath God chosen, yea, and things which are not, to bring to nought things that are:

[29]"That no flesh should glory in his presence" (1 Corinthians 1:25-29).

Fasting is foolishness to many but, to God, it is his wisdom to overcoming and mortifying the flesh.

Oh, how we need to practice the mystery of God.

"always bearing about in the body the dying of the lord Jesus, that the life also of Jesus might be made manifest in our body. [11] For we which live are always delivered unto death for Jesus' sake, that the life also of Jesus might be made manifest in our mortal flesh" (2 Corinthians 4:10).

Fasting brings about the sacrifice required to manifest the life of Jesus in our lives.

The Mystery of Fasting

"Having therefore these promises, dearly beloved, let us cleanse ourselves from all filthiness of the flesh and spirit, perfecting holiness in the fear of God" (2 Corinthians 7:1).

"[16] this I say then, walk in the spirit, and ye shall not fulfil the lust of the flesh.

[17] for the flesh lusteth against the spirit, and the spirit against the flesh: and these are contrary the one to the other: so that ye cannot do the things that ye would.

[18] But if ye be led of the spirit, ye are not under the law.

[19] Now the works of the flesh are manifest, which are these; adultery, fornication, uncleanness, lasciviousness,

[20] Idolatry, witchcraft, hatred, variance, emulations, wrath, strife, seditions, heresies,

[21] *Envyings, murders, drunkenness, revellings, and such like: of the which I tell you before, as I have also told you in time past, that they which do such things shall not inherit the kingdom of God*" (Galatians 5:16-21).

Fasting is walking in the spirit.

We will not have the rule of the kingdom in our lives by walking in the flesh.

In fact, when you realize these things in you, it's your spirit most likely leading you to fast and put your body under subjection by allowing your spirit to lead and be strengthened.

"the blueness of a wound cleanseth away evil: so, do stripes the inward parts of the belly" (Proverbs 20:30).

Proverbs is alluding to fasting here. Fasting, cleanses the inward parts of the soul from the manifestation of the flesh.

"[19] Wherefore, my beloved brethren, let every man be swift to hear, slow to speak, slow to wrath:

[20] For the wrath of man worketh not the righteousness of God.

[21] Wherefore lay apart all filthiness and superfluity of naughtiness, and receive with meekness the engrafted word, which is able to save your souls.

[22] But be ye doers of the word, and not hearers only, deceiving your own selves.

[23] *For if any be a hearer of the word, and not a doer, he is like unto a man beholding his natural face in a glass"* (James 1:19-23).

Nathaniel McNeil

Anger and the like are rampant.
The church today exhibits the same fleshly manifested things as the world. How are we leaders or to lead people to Christ?
When we hear the word God and do true self-examination, it is like a person looking in the mirror and getting a true picture of themselves.
Ask yourself honestly right now, do you look like what God has revealed through his word?
If not, your spirit is leading you to fast.
We must understand that we live in two worlds. The spirit, which is eternal, and the physical world, of which Satan is the God of it. Fasting gives us access to the deeper things of the eternal world.

7

SUPERNATURAL LAWS OF FASTING

The principle of fasting is the law, policy, rule or direction God gave to us for power. Just as a law must be respected if one is to operate on the earth, likewise, faith is a law of the spiritual realm to access heavenly things on earth. Let us have a glance on several principles of fasting.

There are two main overriding principles related to fasting in the Bible.

First, biblical fasting is going without food. The noun translated "fast" is "**tsom**" in the Hebrew and "**nesteia**" in the Greek language. It means the voluntary abstinence from food. The literal Hebrew translation would be "to put no food in the mouth or not to eat." The literal Greek means "no food." I know people who say that they go without television or movies, and they call these "fasting" times. I'm not opposed to that definition of fasting—fasting does imply that we are giving up one thing to replace it with something else, BUT, in the Bible sense, fasting is abstaining from food and individually to replace other things with prayer. But in the main sense, I believe fasting has to do with our abstaining from food. Second, biblical fasting is linked to serious seasons of worship. The more seriously we approach fasting---the more serious the results we will experience.

I sometimes hear people say, "I'm giving up chocolate," and they regard this as a type of fasting. I think this is a somewhat frivolous approach. The first and foremost purpose of a biblical or spiritual fast is to get a breakthrough on a matter that one lifts to the Lord in prayer. A holy fast involves our hearts and the way in which we relate to and trust God. It relates to discerning and receiving strength to follow through on what God might reveal to us about circumstances in our lives or a direction we are to take. I am not against people fasting to lose weight. Many people fast to lose weight or maintain their weight. What I am opposed to is making the loss of weight your primary goal in a season of spiritual fasting. To have weight loss as a goal makes your fasting a diet plan, not a time of spiritual fasting. If losing weight is your purpose in fasting, you will be missing out on the full reason for fasting, and you likely will be concerned only with what you don't eat rather than with what you are led to pray about.

Now there's certainly an issue of food that is associated with many seasons of fasting. To gain control of your eating is a valid reason to fast. The purpose is not the number of pounds you might lose during a fast, but rather, trusting God to help you regain mastery over food during a fast. Jesus said, "The spirit is willing, but the flesh is weak" (Matt. 26:41). Fasting is a means of bringing the flesh into submission unto the Lord so that He strengthens us in our mastery over ourselves. Fasting in the flesh makes us stronger to stand against the temptations of the flesh. Those temptations very often deal with food. Abstaining from food is often God's way of showing that His desire for us is that we regain mastery over all things associated with our flesh to subdue our flesh and elevate our emphasis on spiritual matters. God promises to help us as we overcome the flesh and put all carnal temptations into subjection.

ABSTAINING FROM FOOD TO REGAIN MASTERY OF THE FLESH

We are wise to recognize that food was the enticement the devil used to cause Eve and Adam to sin in the Garden of Eden. In Genesis 2, the Lord God told Adam and Eve that they could eat freely of every tree in the Garden of Eden, "but of the tree of the knowledge of good and evil, thou shalt not eat of it: for in the day that thou eatest thereof thou shalt surely die" (Genesis 2:17). God did not tell Adam and Eve to refrain from touching a specific animal or smelling a specific flower or swimming in a specific stream. He told them to refrain from taking a certain fruit into their bodies—one type of fruit out of all the many types He had made available to them.

God gave Adam and Eve authority over all things that He had created—every bird, fish, beast of the field, and over "every herb bearing seed, which is upon the face of all the earth, and every tree, in which is the fruit of a tree yielding seed; to you it shall be for meat" (Genesis 1:29). God did not prohibit Adam and Eve from interacting with any part of God's creation when He commanded them to be fruitful, multiply, replenish the earth, and subdue it—except for this one tree and its fruit. They were not to eat of a specific tree, what God described to them as the "tree of the knowledge of good and evil." Why did God set apart this one tree and its fruit? God was giving Adam and Eve free will and the ability to make choices and decisions. Free will isn't free if a person has no choice.

Adam and Eve had a choice to make about this one tree. God told them to abstain from eating from its fruit because He did not want His beloved creation to know evil. He had already given them a full knowledge of everything He called "good." He wanted to spare them the heartache of knowing evil. That's true for us today as Christians. God calls us to pursue what is good. Paul wrote to the Philippians:

"Whatsoever things are true... honest... just... pure... lovely... of good report; if there be any virtue, and if there be any praise, think on these things" (Philippians 4:8). God desires only good for His children. He tells us in His Word, "Be not overcome of evil but overcome evil with good" (Romans 12:21). Even as God calls us away from evil and toward good, He gives us a choice. So many of the problems we have in our world today are the result of men and women making the wrong choices. They have knowingly and unknowingly chosen what is evil. And the result is the same for us as it was for Adam and Eve: death and all forms of sin that lead to death (see Romans 6:23).

Let's look at two results from the disastrous choice that Adam and Eve made about the fruit of the tree of knowledge of good and evil.

Diverted Attention

First, Eve listened to what the devil had to say to her about the fruit itself. The devil diverted her attention from whatever she was doing. He called her attention to the tree. The Bible tells us that the devil came to her in the guise of a beautiful and subtle serpent and said to her, "Hath God said, Ye shall not eat of every tree of the garden?" (Genesis 3:1). There's no indication that Eve had given much thought to the tree before the devil asked her this question. There's no record that she longed for it or had any curiosity about it. She certainly didn't crave it, because she had never tasted it!

In many ways, the devil uses this same tactic today. He calls our attention to how beautiful and refreshing certain foods and beverages appear. It's difficult to go through a day without seeing

The Mystery of Fasting

enticing food and beverage commercials on billboards, on television, and in magazines. Foods are presented in the most attractive ways in stores, restaurants, and on menus. The devil says the same thing to us as he said to Eve: "Has God said you couldn't have a bite of this?" A woman once said to me, "If there's a piece of pie in my house, it calls out to me. It says to me, even in the middle of the night, 'Eat me. I can't resist!" Now, I'm certainly not linking the devil to that piece of pie, but I am saying this: The devil will always call your attention repeatedly to the thing that is harmful to you. He will do it in a way that makes you feel deprived if you don't indulge in eating, drinking, or partaking of what is harmful. The implication of the devil is always: "This is so good. Has God said you couldn't have any of this good thing?"

Never forget that the fruit of the tree of the knowledge of good and evil was the knowledge of good and evil. There was an element of good in that fruit, not just evil. The devil told Eve specifically that the fruit of the tree was "good for food, and that it was pleasant to the eyes" (Genesis 3:6). All Eve had to do was look to see that the fruit was pleasant. She made a bad assumption, however, that was what visually pleasant would also be—"good for food." In that, the devil was wrong! What about us? There's an element of good in foods and substances that are ultimately bad for us, even if it's just the excellent appearance, smell, or taste. Have you ever noticed how beautiful all the colored and distinctly shaped bottles look in a bar? Those bottles always seem light in just the right way to make them look very special, very festive, very appealing. Many foods are pleasant to the eyes. Many drinks are presented in ways that make them appear pleasing. We buy into the lie that what is pleasing is also nutritious and beneficial.

Fasting calls for us to turn away from food and redivert our attention back to the things of God and His commandments. Fasting calls, us to face and overcome the devil's call: "Has God said you couldn't have this?" Fasting calls for us to abstain from all things harmful to us, and in most cases, from all food for a period. The devil's insistent question is likely to become very loud in our minds as we begin a fast: "Has God said you couldn't eat?

Not anything? Not the things that you love the most? Has God called you to fast—to abstain totally from this thing that you have labeled as 'good'?"

Our answer must be a firm "Yes! God has called me to fast. He has called me to give my full attention to Him and His commandments. He has called me to obey Him fully in all things. And God has called me to say no to you, Devil!"

2. Temptations Toward False Benefits

Eve listened to what the devil had to say to her about the benefits of eating what God had prohibited. I often wondered why eve would listen to the devil until I looked closer at Genesis 3:1. In this verse, the word serpent in Hebrew is rendered "**nachash**" which means whisperer, enchanter as a sorcerer. The root of this Hebrew word nachash means to shine, which means a shining one. The Chaldea uses this word to mean brass to represent its shining ability. In Isaiah 14: 12 the devil is given a title, Lucifer. Lucifer means light-bearer, morning star. In Ezekiel 28: 13,14 and 17, it reveals that his beauty contributed to his light. Understand these are titles that describe the devil, but as for his actual name, we are not told in Scripture. But in Luke 10:18, Jesus says: "He beheld Satan's fall as lightning from heaven." Lastly, Paul in 2 Corinthians 11: 3 and 14 speaks of Satan as an angel of light. As we look further into this text, we see that in Genesis 3:1 that the serpent was more subtle than any other beast of the field. Beast in

Hebrew is **"chay"** which means living creature. Thus, Satan is wiser and prudent than any other living creature he created. Further, Ezekiel 28 tells us he possessed great wisdom. Thus, Eve was not in the presence of just a mere animal that spoke no much greater. Eve had some type of awe for this being we know as the serpent. In other words, Satan can appear as light, though he is a liar. When he appears as light, he does so to deceive. The devil always points out the would be and usually short-term benefits of sin. Many substances that are ultimately harmful to us taste good or feel good or bring pleasure. In some cases, the partaking of the material makes us feel like adults, feel accepted by others, or feel

The Mystery of Fasting

more powerful and in greater control. Some people say about certain foods and substances that they "give me quick energy," "make me more alert," or "help me relax."

The devil told Eve that the fruit from the tree of the knowledge of good and evil would make her wise—she would be as a **"god,"** knowing good and evil.

In the short term, the devil was right. Eve suddenly knew evil. She knew in her own experience as a human being that evil existed. This was the first time in her life she had ever known the contrast—up to that point; all things had been good.

What the devil failed to mention to Eve was the ultimate consequence that God had associated with eating of this fruit: **"You shall surely die."** The devil failed to mention any downside to her disobedience. He dismissed God's consequences with a sarcastic question.

The devil comes at us the same way. The devil never tells us that drinking alcohol can make a person an alcoholic. He never tells a person that smoking cigarettes can cause him or her to have lung cancer. He never tells a person that overeating of the wrong foods can lead to chronic illness and premature death. The devil points out only short-term benefits, never the long-term disasters.

When we fast, we are suddenly aware once again of what is good and evil. We have a heightened awareness not only of God's goodness and God's commandments but of the evil that abounds in the world around us.

A man once said to me about fasting, "It seems that when I fast the world seems more black and white, at least for a period. I see right and wrong much more clearly. I see good and bad, blessings and cursing, benefits and negative consequences, what is godly and what is ungodly. I am much more discerning about what lines up with God's commandments and what falls into the category of 'man's commands.'" I asked him what happened after he stopped fasting. He laughed and said, "I am still very clear on these things, but there's also a time after I end fasting that the whole world seems more vivid and more colorful than ever before. I can distinguish tastes again. The sky seems bluer than before. The air seems crisper in the mountains. All of my senses seem to be heightened toward what is God's creation—which is always good—and what is man's invention—which very often has an element of evil to it."

Those who fast often experience greater discernment of good and evil. It seems to be a significant by-product of fasting. God seems to give us an opportunity as we fast to retake a look at our lives and the world around us and to discern what is good and what is evil.

FAITH WE WILL NEED FAITH IN OUR FASTING

"And he said, I will hide my face from them, I will see what their end shall be: for they are a very forward generation, children in whom is no faith" (Deuteronomy 32:20).

"Behold, his soul which is lifted up is not upright in him: but the just shall live by his faith" (Habakkuk 2:4).

God will hide his face even when we fast without faith. Lack of faith is due to pride and idolatry. By not looking unto the fast in the fast, you are standing on the sure words of God during your fast that creates the power. No time for exacting your normal pleasures. This the time for being consumed with the sure word of God which is the faith of God or the word of God. We must fast using the word.

"Even the righteousness of God which is by faith of Jesus Christ unto all and upon all them that believe: for there is no difference" (Romans 3:22):
By the faith of Jesus Christ—the word Christ is the anointed. The word of truth is the anointed. Thus, we are using the anointing of Jesus in the fast as we enter therein by faith.
When we use faith, we are using the anointed one. ***"Therefore, being justified by faith, we have peace with God through our Lord Jesus Christ"*** (Romans 3:1):
"By whom also we have access by faith into this grace wherein we stand and rejoice in hope of the glory of God" (Romans 5:2).
We are declared righteous by faith and we enter the fast in peace with God. We don't enter with the mind to gain power for our own glory and to show for fame, power, prestige, elegance, money, or any other fleshly gain. But we enter the fast based on the finished work of the blood of Christ Jesus. But verse two reveals there is more for us than just being born again and being declared righteous. That we now have access by faith in this grace. Grace in the Greek is ***"charis",*** *it* means to stress the benefits.
Benefits given as a result of the graciousness of God. This grace is the high favor of God—we have access to divine privileges.
Fasting is a divine privilege to access the deeper things of God. These things are kingdom privileges.

"Therefore, as ye abound in everything, in faith, and utterance, and knowledge, and in all diligence, and in your love to us, see that ye abound in this grace also" (2 Corinthians 8:7).
We will abound, succeed, and access manifestations of the deeper things and advance in the kingdom by using faith.
So fasting needs faith to abound, succeed what is intensely desired.
"This only would I learn of you, Received ye the Spirit by the works of the law, or by the hearing of faith" (Galatians 3:2)?

The Mystery of Fasting

"He therefore that ministereth to you the Spirit, and worketh miracles among you, doeth he it by the works of the law, or by the hearing of faith" (Galatians 3:5)?

"Know ye therefore that they which are of faith, the same are the children of Abraham" (Galatians 3:7).
Fasting isn't done by works. In fact, it isn't works. It's a faith tool that only brings results by faith.
Faith is imperative and essential when fasting.
It is how we access the full benefits of the covenants.
"For unto us was the gospel preached, as well as unto them: but the word preached did not profit them, not being mixed with faith in them that heard it" (Hebrews 4:2).
When you don't receive the benefits of fasting it is because you didn't mix the fast with faith.
Fasting is a blessing but will only profit as we mix it with faith.
We can only draw near to God by using faith.
"Let us draw near with a true heart in full assurance of faith, having our hearts sprinkled from an evil conscience, and our bodies washed with pure water" (Hebrews 10:22).
When we fast and draw near to God, we must do it with faith.

"But without faith it is impossible to please him: for he that cometh to God must believe that he is, and that he is a rewarder of them that diligently seek him" (Hebrews 11:6).
Our fasting will not please God without faith... point blank, you can't do anything with God or in God without faith.
He rewards diligent seekers who have faith.
Therefore, many fast but get no results because they fast without faith. Your fast is rewarded by using faith.

"Whom God hath set forth to be a propitiation through faith in his blood, to declare his righteousness for the remission of sins that are past, through the forbearance of God" (Romans 3:25);

"Where is boasting then? It is excluded. By what law? of works? Nay: but by the law of faith" (Romans 3:27).

"Do we then make void the law through faith? God forbid: yea, we establish the law" (Romans 3:31).

We use the sure word of God in the fast to establish that what we pray for is sure according to the word of God.

So, then we must know what faith is and to use it in the fast for it to be successful.

Faith—what exactly is faith?

Many believe faith is just believing, but faith is a noun not a verb.

Faith is a thing that moves us to action.

Car is a noun—drive is a verb.

If you're going to use a car, you don't say to someone, "I'm going to car to the store." But you say "drive the car to the store" because the car is a thing and driving an action.

So, it is with faith…

The Hebrew word for faith is emunah—it means firmness. But it is literal firmness, stability, security, and truth.

So, faith is truth…

The root word is emuwn—which is established truth.

Truth is a noun not a verb…

Truth that is sure and secure can only come from God for his word is sure.

"The law of the LORD is perfect, converting the soul: the testimony of the LORD is sure, making wise the simple" (Psalm 19:7).

"Thy testimonies are very sure: holiness becometh thine house, O LORD, forever" (Psalm 93:5).

"The works of his hands are verity and judgment; all his commandments are sure" (Psalm 111:7).

The Mystery of Fasting

Emunah is from the root word emuwn, which means the established truth...

Faith is, thus, established truth or simply truth. When we speak or carry truth, we are carrying the Godkind of language. Faith is truth, revelation of truth, the words of truth, or divine information. Well, what is truth? The communication and reception of knowledge, intelligence, or instruction.

"[1] LORD, who shall abide in thy tabernacle? who shall dwell in thy holy hill? [2] He that walketh uprightly, and worketh righteousness, and speaketh the truth in his heart" (Psalm 15:1-2). Truth is what God is—we worship him in spirit and truth. To have God's words in our hearts is to have the faith of God in our hearts...

"And the woman said to Elijah, Now by this I know that thou art a man of God, and that the word of the LORD in thy mouth is truth" (1 Kings 17:24).

"Withhold not thou thy tender mercies from me, O LORD: let thy lovingkindness and thy truth continually preserve me" (Psalm 40:11).

"O send out thy light and thy truth: let them lead me; let them bring me unto thy holy hill, and to thy tabernacles" (Psalm 43:3).

"Thou hast given a banner to them that fear thee, that it may be displayed because of the truth. Selah" (Psalm 60:4).

Your fast will display wonders because of the truth.
Faith is truth!!!

"He shall cover thee with his feathers, and under his wings shalt thou trust: his truth shall be thy shield and buckler" (Psalm 91:4).

His truth or faith will be your shield and buckler... buckler means something that surrounds and defends you.
Faith is what will shield and surround you to defend against the attacks while you fast.

"Justice and judgment are the habitation of thy throne: mercy and truth shall go before thy face" (Psalm 89:14).

Only coming before the lord with truth or faith ...

We can't come into his presence without faith... in fact, we show before his face with faith...

God's truth being known as divine information is acquired by studying and prayer.

Fasting requires we read and study the word or listen to the word and spiritual lessons. It is feeding ourselves with a diet of nothing but the word of God.

Truth is also a guarantee—the assurance of fulfilment of a condition.

The word of God secures the promises, privileges spoken of in whisper word.

It is our inheritance. What we can be sure to expect from the word for our lives.

Example: our bank cards are our guarantee of our money in the bank. When you're not sure what's on the card you may call.

When you call, after you give them the proper information, you find out how much is in the bank. Once you know, when you go to the bank machine, you have assurance you may get up to that amount.

At this point, you're not trying to believe that this is yours, but you have evidence, surety...

Well, God's word must be treated as such. When you read, it is truth. It is sure. If all the bank computers shut down, that's ok, because God's word must still provide for us.

Fasting brings rewards. That's all you need to know now that you're within the fast and see what God does.

Now faith is the substance of things hoped for, the evidence of things not seen" (Hebrews 11:1).

Faith in the Greek is "**pistis**". It is a noun not action, but it will produce action.

Pistis—divine information that produces obedience.

Faith is invisible but tangible and real. Obedience is the action produced from the faith received. Faith is the word of God with the significance of produced conviction.

"[8] But what saith it? The word is nigh thee, even in thy mouth, and in thy heart: that is, the word of faith, which we preach;".

The Mystery of Fasting

[14] How then shall they call on him in whom they have not believed? and how shall they believe in him of whom they have not heard? and how shall they hear without a preacher?

[15] And how shall they preach, except they be sent? as it is written, How beautiful are the feet of them that preach the gospel of peace and bring glad tidings of good things!

[16] But they have not all obeyed the gospel. For Esaias saith, Lord, who hath believed our report?

[17] So, then faith cometh by hearing, and hearing by the word of God" (Romans 10:8, 14-17).

Faith is the word of God! Period.

The word for "word" here is **"rhema"** in the Greek which means living word.

Rhema—a word, not all the entire scriptures, but to an individual. Divine truths and information which the spirit of God brings to us or opens to us as we need it.

Thus, faith is God's word alive in us that produces actions. All we need is the mustard seed faith that grows.

"But what saith it? The word is nigh thee, even in thy mouth, and in thy heart: that is, the word of faith, which we preach" (Romans 10:8).

The word of faith here is the rhema. Rhema—a portion of the word fitting our lives. Whenever Jesus fasted, he constantly dealt with the enemy using the word of God.

He used the portion needed at that time. Fasting requires the Word. You need to be present in your life. Fasting requires faith to faith to faith.

"For therein is the righteousness of God revealed from faith to faith: as it is written, The just shall live by faith" (Romans 1:17).

We must live by the rhema or words of faith.

Nathaniel McNeil

9

HOW TO FAST

Fasting is a sacred time in which Christians abstain from food or other pleasures and take the time to focus on God. We fast with faith, prayer, praise, and giving. Along with not eating, we incorporate the mysteries of faith, prayer and praise and mourning. Though these are all mysteries on how they work, we know from Scripture they work. Fasting must be done correctly. Knowing the purpose of fasting is part of fasting effectively. The medical information on fasting is taken from Christian physician, Don Colbert's book on "Toxic Relief". To know more detail about what is medically shared here, I recommend getting a copy of this book to get an even greater understanding.

If you are diagnosed with a disease or infirmity, I also suggest that you not go on an extended fast without first going over this with your personal care physician.

To understand that living a fasted life [or fasting more frequently] howbeit, weekly or monthly for a period of time, you must take into consideration your health and avoid any potential problems. Living a fasted life is reserved for those who understand that they were born for a great and special purpose. You understand that your life is not your own and you live each day in complete devotion to God. It's this type of believer who desires to influence cities and entire nations for the Lord and will put their flesh under, bringing its cravings and desires under the subjection of their spirit man in order to make the greatest impact that they can. At the same time, it's been medically proven that fasting can effectively help improve medical conditions from colds and flu to heart disease. It's also beneficial for hypertension, allergies, asthma, and even type two diabetes.

There are times when it's recommended that you do not fast. Among those times you should not fast if you're pregnant or nursing, malnourished, have AIDS, cancer, before or after surgery, as it could interfere with your ability to heal after surgery. In addition, don't fast if you have cardiac arrhythmia or congestive heart failure, mental illness including depression, anxiety, schizophrenia, and bipolar disease, as well as severe liver and kidney disease. Some conditions could worsen when you fast. Again, if you have an illness, please contact your personal care physician before beginning a regimen of fasting.

There are two portions of Scripture that come into play as we consider the medical effects and medical aspect of fasting. The first thing you must never do is place medical opinions above God. Doctors have been given by God and have been given the privilege of having insight into the mechanics of the human body and how it functions.

They can treat certain conditions and because of their instruction, the lives of many people have been spared and extended many years. It is wisdom for our generation to avail ourselves to the doctor's advice and extend our lives as long as possible to fulfill God's purpose.

However, the caution is to not place more trust in a doctor than in God. Proverbs Chapter 3 says:

[1] My son, do not forget my law, but let your heart keep my commands; [2] For length of days and long life and peace they will add to you. [3] Let not mercy and truth forsake you; Bind them around your neck, write them on the tablet of your heart,
[4] And so, find favor and high esteem in the sight of God and man.
[5] Trust in the Lord with all your heart, and lean not on your own understanding;
[6] In all your ways acknowledge Him, and He shall direct your paths.

The Word of God is still to be the final authority in your fasting decisions and when it comes to adjusting your life to what advice your doctor gives, you must always consider the Word of God and

The Mystery of Fasting

keep the commands of God in your heart. The result is a long life of peace in the earth.

Therefore, you must trust in the Lord with all your heart and acknowledge Him in what you do whether it's a lifestyle adjustment to lose weight, preventative medicines, or an operation. The Lord is the Great Physician and He always knows what's best.

The second portion of Scripture is also found in Proverbs. God never intends for us to be ignorant of the things that have been made available to us. A mistake that some believers make is to forsake the knowledge that God has given us through medical professionals. They associate someone that may go to a doctor as being in doubt or unbelief or not trusting God.

They continue to argue that you should not even seek the advice of a doctor and trust God for a miracle. Although I agree that we should always trust God for and expect a miracle, this mindset is not scriptural. You can associate the above mindset with the children of Israel as they wandered in the wilderness for forty years. The Lord was their doctor and they experienced miracle after miracle.

Using the miracle of the Manna and Quail as an example, the Lord provided both supernaturally, however, when the children of Israel entered the land that God promised them, Joshua 5:11, 12 says,

"[11] And they ate of the produce of the land on the day after the Passover, unleavened bread and parched grain, on the very same day.

[12] Then the manna ceased on the day after they had eaten the produce of the land; and the children of Israel no longer had manna, but they ate the food of the land of Canaan that year."

The wisdom of God is shown in us when we mature and learn what has been made available to us in the land we live. Some people continue to trust God for miracles when the provision for their need has already been made.

God expects us to use our brains to sustain and lengthen our lives while we live in the earth. Proverbs chapter 4 says:

[7] Wisdom is the principal thing; Therefore, get wisdom. And in all your getting, get understanding.

[8] Exalt her, and she will promote you; She will bring you honor, when you embrace her.
[9] She will place on your head an ornament of grace; a crown of glory she will deliver to you.
[10] Hear, my son, and receive my sayings, and the years of your life will be many.
[11] I have taught you in the way of wisdom; I have led you in right paths.
[12] When you walk, your steps will not be hindered, and when you run, you will not stumble.
[13] Take firm hold of instruction, do not let go; Keep her, for she is your life.

The natural laws of fasting are part of your tapping into the wisdom and understanding the Lord has given to us through doctors.

Starting and ending a fast properly can keep you from experiencing many things that we often associate with fasting, from headaches to constipation. These things are shared to make our fasting as pleasurable an experience as possible.

Whatever physical benefits we may receive as a result of entering a lifestyle of spiritual fasting will entail a change in lifestyle when the fast is over. It must be understood that whatever physical infirmity you may face, it was most likely due to harmful habits of eating or living. Therefore, there must be a reformation in your habits, or the physical benefits of fasting will not take hold in your life and will remain elusive.

What I mean is unless we're willing to adjust how much we eat, the foods we consume, and how we live, we may struggle with some ailments that God never intended.

Whether you're healthy or not you need to get the mind of God before undertaking a fast, especially a prolonged fast of more than three days. Just as importantly, you need to be certain that your motives are clear and make certain that whatever you may hope to gain in health and healing, that the spiritual purposes of God will prevail, and the benefits of health would be an added benefit to your life and walk with God.

Acknowledge the Lord as you begin your fast and get the mind of God. Then, utilize wisdom as you pray and meditate frequently during this time.

THINGS TO CONSIDER WHEN FASTING

1.   Have a clear aim. You must not think fasting is only a method for people to cultivate their religious instinct. When you fast, you must have a clear objective; if you do not, you will become distracted and disinterested and fail to continue. Each of us is faced with many problems such as our relationship with God, our personality, harmony in the family, health, business problems, financial problems, and other such things. Usually, only the most urgent issues are brought before God in fasting.

Daniel mourned, partially fasted three weeks beseeching God to deliver the Israelites from distress. King David fasted multiple times and received multiple vivid visions and revelations of the messiah. Elijah fasted for forty days to save Israel. Many times, in the history of the nation of Israel, the kings and the people fasted to repent and receive deliverance. Even the king of Nineveh, when he heard God was going to destroy the city, repented and the people of that city fasted for three days. Our Lord Jesus Christ fasted forty days in the wilderness to prepare Himself for public ministry. We should also have a definite aim and purpose for our fasting. If someone feels that he does not have a reason for fasting, let him be careful, because the very fact that he thinks he has no problem is often an indication of one. It may be that in his arrogant mind he feels self-sufficient and in no need of help. This is a severe problem.

We Christians today have many things about which to pray. We can get up early in the morning and think over our lives and our society. As we meditate, we will become aware of many things we need to fast. If one tries to fast without a clear aim, he is as a child without conviction, not knowing his mind. It is essential for the believer to fast with a clear aim and definite purpose.

2. **Do not fast for a show.** In the Gospel of Matthew, it is written: "Moreover when ye fast, be not, as the hypocrites, of a sad countenance: for they disfigure their faces, that they may appear unto men to fast. Verily I say unto you; They have their reward. But thou, when thou fastest, anoint thine head and wash thy face; that thou appear not unto men to fast, but unto thy Father which is in secret: and thy Father, which seeth in secret shall reward thee openly" (Matthew 6:16-18).

Occasionally, a person will take pride in his fasting. To fast for a week, ten days, or more is a beautiful thing but also very difficult. We should remember that we are fasting not unto men but God. Therefore, our fasting must be done in secret and humbly before Him. If one boasts about his fasting, the Holy Spirit cannot work, and nothing is accomplished. Before we begin to fast, we must learn to come to Him humbly and in the proper attitude, not just to appear holy unto men.

3. **Overcome the temptation** of being boastful and proud. The devil will tempt us to fast for show unto men or even for show unto God. Most people begin their fast in humility and with a definite aim. But as the days pass by, there is a great temptation to become proud in spirit and to fast for the show.

If you begin to think, "I have fasted for this long, so God must answer me," beware, as this IS a danger signal that Satan is tempting you in this regard. Your fasting does not obligate God to fulfill all of your heart's desires.

We must realize that God will not forgive our sins because of our fasting. All are sinners and by our efforts cannot receive pardon even though we fast for many days. We can receive forgiveness of sin only by the power of the shed blood of His only begotten Son. What is the necessity of fasting? Fasting is a time during which we deny ourselves and invite the power of the Holy Spirit into our hearts, yielding our will to the will of God. Even after we are saved by grace, the temptation to sin still exists. We must resist these temptations of Satan and yield to the supernatural power of God. When we fast humbly before God, our old carnal nature is crucified, and then the power of the Holy Spirit is manifested in our lives. Diseases are healed, impossible problems solved, and peace and harmony are restored in our hearts and homes.

The Mystery of Fasting

We cannot receive the power of God through our efforts through fasting. When our sexual nature is in subjection, and we come humbly before the Throne of Grace, we can be filled with the power of God. As our spirit is restored, we can worship Him in spirit and truth. The power of God is always waiting for our surrendered invitation. This is an important principle that we must understand when we begin to fast.

Sometimes, pride will surface when fasting is discussed. There are those who are proud of their previous long fasts. Upon meeting a person who has only a little experience in fasting, they will piously remark how they fasted for three weeks and state that one cannot understand the meaning of fasting until they have fasted for at least ten days. To speak boastfully of the length of a fast is to manifest the spirit of pride.

4. Plan your time during the fast. There is a necessary procedure involved in fasting besides that which deals with the physical aspects previously mentioned. This involves our faith and belief. Most people who fast begin fervently to read the Bible and pray. But one or two days later, they find themselves unduly concerned about how they are going to be able to complete the period that they decided to fast. When you choose a certain length of time, divide the fast into three parts.

Spend the first part repenting of your sins and examining yourself honestly and openly before God. This time cannot be a prescribed number of days but varies with each. As you pray, the Holy Spirit will show you your sins; even some you may not know exists.

Spend the second part making your petition before the Throne of Grace. We must honestly examine our aim in the light of the Holy Spirit and determine if that aim is indeed the will of God. As you discover this, you must not be discouraged but steadfastly continue to pray, support your prayers with the reading of God's Word. This builds your faith.

The third part is the period to have firm belief in one's prayers. Remember, God's power is mighty. He does not turn His face away when His children come in prayer. This convinces us that God has answered our prayers. Visualize the answer and transfer faith into action. The Bible says, "What things soever ye desire, when ye pray, believe that ye receive them, and ye shall have them" (Mark 11:24).

God cannot use you if your faith in yourself is as big as a mountain, but when you realize that you are nothing and your faith in Christ is the size of a mustard seed, then He will miraculously remove the mountains in your life. God can use this faith for us. Just as a small piece of yeast raises a whole loaf of bread, so God will use our little hope to increase our faith so that it will permeate all our actions. The moment we firmly believe that God has answered, we invite the power of God into our life. It is necessary to express our faith with praise and thankfulness to God for what He has done. Indeed, He does exceedingly, abundantly above all that we can ask or even think. The fact that we are convinced that God has answered is the key to the establishment and maintaining of our relationship with God.

5.   Fasting bring about a change in us. The purpose of fasting is not only to receive healing, guidance, and solutions to severe problems. Fasting is to access the deeper things of God given by virtue of our being born again. To access the powers of the kingdom of God; you must be born again, accept Christ as your Savior and let Him fill your heart. What does it mean to be born again?

One day a man named Nicodemus came to Jesus and asked the way to eternal life. Then Jesus answered him, "Verily, verily, I say unto thee, Except a man be born again, he cannot see the kingdom of God" (John 3:3). How can one be born the second time? We must not only be born physically, but we must be born of the Spirit. We can be changed by the power of the Spirit of God. After this happens, our whole life, attitudes, thoughts, and speech is altered. As we yield all to Christ, He will baptize us in the Holy Ghost and fire. We then receive power to live an overcoming life and have a greater love for the Word of God, a more profound respect for others, and an intensified burden for the lost. The initial evidence of this filling is the fluent speaking in an unknown language that we have never studied. If we remain in the same spiritual condition after our fast as before, there is no effect. There are those who fast for fasting itself or achieve some special purpose or recognition. This is a misunderstanding of the use of

The Mystery of Fasting

fasting. Fasting will make a constitutional change in our physical makeup, but the primary goal is that our nature changed. We must clean out every type of sin in our heart that has been accumulating. The supernatural power of God, which stands above science through the blood of Jesus Christ causes a miraculous change as we allow it.

6.   We must not make fasting. When we fast for one day or even a hundred days, that would not add up to one small righteous or meritorious deed before God unless we are holy. The prophet Zechariah said that we must fast to give glory and honor to God. And then he said, "Thus speaketh the Lord of hosts, saying, Execute true judgment, and show mercy and compassions every man to his brother: and oppress not the widow, nor the fatherless, the stranger, nor the poor; and let none of you imagine evil against his brother in your heart" (Zechariah 7:9-10).

Also, the prophet Isaiah wrote, "Is it such a fast that I have chosen? A day for a man to afflict his soul? Is it to bow down his head as a bulrush, and to spread sackcloth and ashes under him? Wilt thou call this a fast, and an acceptable day to the Lord? Is not this the fasting that I have chosen? to lose the bands of wickedness, to undo the heavy burdens, and to let the oppressed go free, and that ye break every yoke?" (Isaiah 58:5-7).

These scriptures show us the principle that fasting is not beneficial to us if we do not also obey His words. One who considers himself righteous because he fasts does not understand anything about God's grace.

7.   We must restrain ourselves. It is straightforward for some to slip into physical manifestations during a time of fasting. The Holy Spirit always works decently and in order. Therefore, it is necessary to restrain the human manifestations that might occur. As we genuinely seek the Holy Spirit, He will show us the difference between spiritual and fleshly manifestations. It is impossible for us to differentiate without the help of the Holy Spirit.

The prophet Jeremiah makes a firm statement in Jeremiah 14: 12 to those who allow the flesh to motivate them. "When they fast, I will not hear their cry; and when they offer burnt offering and an oblation, I will not accept them.*" Why is it this way? He tells us*

in verse ten, "Thus have they loved to wander, they have not refrained their feet. Therefore, the Lord doth not accept them." (Jeremiah 14: 10)
Because of their insincerity, they have not refrained their feet, and God does not hear their prayers. When we fast, we must restrain not only our food and drink but also physical manifestations. These seven admonitions concerning fasting is essential guidelines for the one who sincerely wants answers from God. Many receive a miracle from God only to lose it soon after they have completed a time of fasting. We must put into practice the faith we receive to retain it. In this regard, I call your attention to a few points that will be helpful.

1.   Satan tempts us continually. Even after we have finished fasting, God has met our needs, and we are motivated by the Holy Spirit, we are not perfect. We will not be holy or perfect persons until we receive our new bodies in heaven. It must be remembered that we are still at war with Satan and must battle him courageously as we did during the time of fasting. In the Gospel of Luke, we see that after Satan tempted Christ in the wilderness, he did not completely retreat. "He departed from him for a season" (Luke 4: 13). So, even more Satan will continue to tempt us. Anyone who becomes proud because of his fasting will easily fall prey to the temptations of Satan. Many succumb to temptations within less than a year after receiving answers from God through fasting. Satan tempts. With this new power and may ask us to perform miracles and do beautiful things. When this temptation comes, we must not recklessly yield to the enticing words of Satan but be humble before God so that He alone will give the victory. Satan will use our adventurous spirit to bring us to a place where the Holy Spirit cannot use us. We can keep humble before God only as we continue to pray daily and study the Word of God.

2.   Recognize our weakness. Even though we fast, as long as we are in this fleshly body, we are still weak. It is the Spirit of God who is strong and not us. Often Christian friends will look up to you as a strong Christian after you have fasted for an extended period, and Satan tempts you to be proud of your reputation. This temptation must also be overcome. If miracles happen under your ministry, Satan will tell you that it is your power that is causing these things to happen. We cannot do any of these miraculous things in ourselves. It is only in the power of the Holy Spirit. We are all sinners and are as clay vessels that are easily broken. We can only wait on the power of the Holy Spirit.

3.   Maintain a positive attitude of faith. After a time of fasting, it is straightforward to become critical of the pastor's sermons, of a friend's Christian life, administration of the church, or other situations. When this happens, we lose the grace and love we have received from God. After earnestly seeking Christ our heart is changed. Only through continually seeking Him will it remain changed thereby allowing us to serve the Lord more diligently than before. We will open our hearts to the teaching of the pastor and do all we can to help carry the burden of the work of God and the church.

As we cast off our negative attitudes, the love of Christ flows through us. This enables us to enjoy a positive Christian life. We must do everything we possibly can to share the message of salvation through the blood of Christ to a lost and dying world. This is the commission we have received from Christ Himself. A negative attitude produces a negative life. Considering that we can do anything through Christ Jesus and live each day in real faith.

MAXIMIZING FASTING

Many fast but do not do it correctly and, thus, never see the spiritual results of fasting. I will share the purpose and what is needed to fast to obtain spiritual results desired. First, we must understand that fasting is not to abuse the body or for physical discomfort, but for the denying of the flesh in order to be filled with the light of God. Fasting must be consciously viewed as a blessing and not a task. We must also know that fasting is for now.

We are in the days of fasting right now. Fasting is the price of power and breaking every yoke. Every single yoke in your life will be broken when our fasting is by the Word of God. Fasting is the price we pay for unlimited power for our spirit man. Power is a value. Nothing of value is free.

Jesus once said this when he was questioned about why his disciples did not fast.

"Can the friends of the bridegroom mourn as long as the bridegroom is with them? But the days will come when the bridegroom will be taken away from them, and then they will fast" (Matthew 9:15). According to the Bible, a fast is a voluntary abstinence from all forms of food and drink, and at the same time, it must be accompanied with prayers and study of God's Word. In the event of a long fast, in the case of Moses and Jesus, consumption of water is assumed, because it is physically impossible to withstand forty days and nights without food and water. (If one were to read Wikipedia's entry on survival skill, a person generally could only survive 3-5 days without water.) Fasting is a voluntary affliction to the soul, for someone to humble in the presence of the Lord, and to make his supplication before God. Fasting is a severe act and is always done with reverence for God. Like the Psalmist said.

"But as for me, when they were sick, My clothing was sackcloth; I humbled myself with fasting, and my prayer would return to my own heart" (Psalm 35:13). – David

"Because zeal for Your house has eaten me up, And the objections of those who reproach You have fallen on me. When I wept and chastened my soul with fasting, That became my reproach" (Psalm 69:9-10). –David

> ***"But You, O GOD the Lord,***
> ***Deal with me for Your name's***
> ***sake;***
> ***Because Your mercy is good, deliver me.***
> ***For I am poor and needy,***
> ***And my heart is wounded within me.***
> ***I am gone like a shadow when it***
> ***lengthens; I am shaken off like a***
> ***locust.***
> ***My knees are weak through fasting,***
> ***And my flesh is feeble from lack of fatness.***

The Mystery of Fasting

I also have become a reproach to them;
When they look at me, they shake their heads"
(Psalm 109:21-25). – David

Although fasting is never recorded in the Mosaic laws of the Old Testament as a law, however, we often see that people like Moses, Samuel, Ezra, Daniel, Cornelius, Peter, and many others fasted. When these Bible characters fasted, God accepted and granted their petitions from time to time according to God's will. Compulsory fasting on a regular basis comes very much later in history and is especially practiced by the Pharisees (Luke 18:11-12), but there are also Godly people who fasted regularly for years, like Anna in Luke 2:36-37.

Is Every Fasting Acceptable before God?

In the earlier discussion, we were looking at the fasting of the Pharisees and the fasting of Anna; we knew that only the latter ones are acceptable to God. Hence, there are fasts that are not acceptable before God.

Isaiah once said on behalf of God.

"Tell My people their transgression, And the house of Jacob their sins. They seek Me daily,
And a delight to know My ways,
As a nation that did righteousness, And did not forsake the ordinance of their God. They ask of Me the ordinances of justice; They take delight in approaching God.
'Why have we fasted,' they say, 'and You have not seen?
Why have we afflicted our souls, and You take no notice?'"
(Isaiah 58:1-3). – Isaiah

God also said through Prophet Zechariah:

"Say to all the people of the land, and to the priests: 'When you fasted and mourned in the fifth and seventh months during those seventy years, did you fast unto Me? When you eat and when you drink, do you not eat and drink for yourselves? Should you not have obeyed the words which the LORD proclaimed through the former prophets when Jerusalem and the cities around it

were inhabited and prosperous, and the South and the Lowland were inhabited?'" (Zechariah 7:4-7). – Zechariah

From here we can see that God didn't always accept the fasting of the people, just like God once turned away the offerings of Cain. Fasting, accompanied with prayers, is also part of our offerings to God and God takes every offering and deed that his children have done in His name seriously.

Like what Jesus said in Matthew 9:15 that there will come a time for Christians to fast and to pray before God. Therefore, it is essential for us to understand what types of fasting pleases God. Just like what Paul encourages believers to offer themselves as a living sacrifice to God, he called that a **"Reasonable Service"** (Romans 12:1). Therefore, it is important for us to ensure that our fasting is acceptable before God and will go up as a memorial before God, just like what the angel of God said to Cornelius "Your prayers and your alms have come up for a memorial before God" (Acts 10:4).

Fasting for the Bridegroom

The disciples of John came to Jesus saying, *"Why do the Pharisees and we fast often, but Your disciples do not fast?" Jesus said to them, "Can the friends of the bridegroom mourn as long as the bridegroom is with them? But the days will come when the bridegroom will be taken away from them, and then they will fast. No one puts a piece of unshrunk cloth on an old garment; for the patch pulls away from the garment, and the tear is made worse. Nor do they put new wine into old wineskins, or else the wineskins break, the wine is spilled, and the wineskins are ruined. But they put new wine into new wineskins, and both are preserved"* (Matthew 9:14-17).

THE DO'S AND DON'TS WHEN FASTING

Do's

1. Constantly Pray to God
Whenever we are fasting, we are bringing request and supplication to God; We must always trust that in God, as well as to pour out all our heart before God (Psalm 62:8). Whenever the disciples would need to get a direction from God, besides fasting, they will always accompany it with prayers (Acts 13:3). Remember, fasting without prayer is just called dieting.

2. Be Thankful and Bold
"Enter his gates with thanksgiving and his courts with praise; give thanks to him and praise his name" (Psalm 100: 4).
"Let us then approach God's throne of grace with confidence, so that we may receive mercy and find grace to help us in our time of need" (Hebrews 4:16).
We must come boldly. We don't beg God, but we begin with boldness. We come before God with the main guarantee that our inheritance in Him can be accessed on the platform of the Name of Jesus.

3. Do Good and Help the Poor
Whenever a Christian fasts, he should always continue to do good and bless the people around, God has one complaint against the fasting of Judah, and he had spoken through Isaiah:
"Is this not the fast that I have chosen:
To loose the bonds of wickedness,

To undo the heavy burdens,
To let the oppressed, go free,
And that you break every yoke?
Is it not to share your bread with the hungry,
And that you bring to your house the poor who are cast out; When you see the naked, that you cover him, And not hide from your flesh?
Then your light shall break forth like the morning,
Your healing shall spring forth speedily,
And your righteousness shall go before you; The glory of the LORD shall be your rear guard.
Then you shall call, and the LORD will answer;
You shall cry, and He will say, 'Here I am"
(Isaiah 58:6-9). – Isaiah

When the Jews were fasting at the time of Isaiah, they continued to oppress the weak, exploit the laborers, and continue their strife and debate among themselves. As a result, God did not want to answer them when they fast and pray. Over here, God is encouraging them to share, and do good to others, only then will God respond to their prayers.

Don'ts

There are a few things that should never be done when you fast.

1. Do not let others know that you are fasting.
"But you, when you fast, anoint your head and wash your face, so that you do not appear to men to be fasting, but to your Father who is in the secret place; and your Father who sees in secret will reward you openly" (Matthew 6:17-18). – Jesus
Jesus encourages Christians to fast, but they should always do this in secret, and not to let another know that he is fasting, God who sees it in secret, will reward openly. **2. Do not fast for the wrong reasons**

The Mystery of Fasting

In the same chapter of Isaiah 58, God spoke through Isaiah the prophet saying:

"Why have we fasted,' they say, 'and You have not seen? Why have we afflicted our souls, and You take no notice?" In fact, on the day of your fast, you find pleasure, And exploit all your laborers. Indeed, you fast for strife and debate, And to strike with the fist of wickedness. You will not fast as you do this day, To make your voice heard on high. Is it a fast that I have chosen, A day for a man to afflict his soul? Is it to bow down his head like a bulrush, And to spread out sackcloth and ashes? Would you call this a fast, And an acceptable day to the LORD?" (Isaiah 58:3-5). – Isaiah

Therefore, let us learn to show reverence to God whenever we fast, let us not fast for the sake of fasting. Let us not fast just because we can't find food for ourselves. Always remember, that God does not look at outer appearance:

"Do not look at his appearance or his physical stature, because I have refused him. For the LORD does not see as man sees; for man looks at the outward appearance, but the LORD looks at the heart" (1 Samuel 16:7).

A biblical example of fasting, and the reason for fasting

To conclude our discussion, I would be quoting examples of fasts that God accepted, and we would draw samples from the Old and New Testaments.

Generally, there are four known reasons why people fast in the Bible

1. To receive power from God

Ô The Lord Jesus himself fasted forty days and forty nights before He started His ministry (Matthew 4:1-2).

Ô The Apostles fasted and prayed with one accord before commissioning and sending out workers (Acts 13:1-3).

Ô Healing and casting out of demons should be carried out through fasting and prayers (Matthew 17:19-21).

2. To request God's help:

Ô Ezra fasted and prayed for Gods protection before starting his trip to Jerusalem (Ezra 8:21-23).

Ô Esther fasted three days and nights before she takes on the risk to see the king (Esther 4:16).

Ô Nehemiah fasted and prayed for God to request for his grace (Nehemiah 1:4-11).

3. To understand the truth:

Ô Daniel mourned and used a restricted diet for the revelation of the things to come (Daniel 10:2-12).

Ô The apostles fasted for God's revelation on the directions to take for ministry (Acts 13:1-2).

4. To confess, repent, and request the forgiveness of sin

Ô The people of Nineveh fasted and repented before God when they heard the preaching of Jonah (Jonah 3:5-10).

Ô The Israelites fasted and confessed their sins and turned to God (1 Samuel 7:3-6).

Ô King Ahab fasted and repented before God when Elijah spoke against him (1 Kings 21:27).

I quoted King Ahab because it is interesting to see that even someone as evil as Ahab, when he genuinely repents before God, God took pity on him and said this through Elijah His prophet: *"See how Ahab has humbled himself before Me? Because he has humbled himself before Me, I will not bring the calamity in his days. In the days of his son, I will bring the calamity to his house"* (2 Kings 21:28). – YHWH This tells us how much fasting does mean to God. But it must be done for the right reasons for God to accept it. Therefore, let us not just fast without a purpose, or else that fasting will fit precisely to what Paul warned the Colossians against.

"Therefore, if you died with Christ from the basic principles of the world, why, as though living in the world, do you subject yourselves to regulations- "Do not touch, do not taste, do not handle, which all concern things which perish with the user according to the commandments and doctrines of men? These things indeed have an appearance of wisdom in self-imposed religion, false humility, and neglect of the body, but are of no value against the indulgence of the flesh" (Colossians 2:20-23). –

The Mystery of Fasting

Paul Therefore, let us keep these principles in mind and to serve God in the way that he would want us to.

Nathaniel McNeil

The Mystery of Fasting

PREPARATION: HOW TO BEGIN A FAST

As you begin this time of fasting, should consider these things in the preparation of your heart prayer, personal reflection, and spiritual growth.
Knowing that you are going to begin a fasting regimen, days before the actual fast, you must do exactly the opposite of what your flesh will tell you. Your flesh says that you are going to deprive yourself of all that good food for one, two, three, and more days, so go and fill up on that steak, potato chips, ice-cream, pie, candy, etc. These are demanding on your digestive system and serve to cause you to crave them more.
Therefore, during this time, you should begin cutting back on this type of food and the portions of foods associated with them. Cut down on the amount of caffeine and sugar you consume in order to reduce or eliminate the headache that's often associated with going on a fast.
Begin eating and enjoying more fresh fruits and vegetables, fruit and vegetable juices, and water. Not only is this healthier for you but will also take a strain off your digestive system and give more energy throughout the day. This in addition makes the transition to fast easier for your body to adjust to once you begin denying it food.
Before you begin, you must set boundaries for your fast. These boundaries may include:

» How long you will pray each day;

» How long you will read the Word each day;

Determine to recommit unsubmitted areas of your life to the Lord as He reveals them. These can include church attendance, church service, obedience in tithing, or sharing the Gospel, as God gives you opportunity.

The purpose for your fast should be defined [if possible]. There have been times when I've been called to a fast and didn't have a clear purpose, only to find out days or even months later the purpose for that fast.

Have a heart of repentance and reconciliation before God by confessing all known sin and having the assurance according to I John chapter 1 that you are reconciled with God and then be reconciled to your fellow man.

During your fast, meditate on Scripture throughout the day, read your Bible and ask the Holy Spirit to give you necessary revelation in whatever area of your life that He wants to.

Listen to Bible teaching tapes and programs as much as you can and in all your spare time. Remember, without including these things in your fast, you are doing little more than going on a diet. Stay focused on the Word of God and pray as often as possible doing whatever the Scripture reveals. Set aside specific time to be quiet before the Lord endeavoring to listen to the voice of the Holy Spirit. Make certain you write down those things He reveals as you don't want them lost two days after having such a powerful encounter with Him.

Write down the prayers you prayed and insight you receive. Also write down any dreams you have and pray for the interpretation they may have [if any].

Allow the Holy Spirit to bring a refreshing to your life as you go through your fast. You can expect mental, physical, and spiritual refreshing and should make this request known to God.

Be mindful of releasing burdens that have attached themselves to you or your loved ones. With this added power in your life, you will be able to be released from the burdens of finances, stress, depression, chronic illness, legal problems, and difficult people. Whatever the burden, ask God for help in these areas.

Be mindful of the power of God in your life that will enable you to be used by Him to bring healing to those that are bruised, those

The Mystery of Fasting

who are under the oppression of the devil and for protection and safety as you and your loved ones go about your daily routines. After the fast, be mindful of the fact that your body is the temple of the Holy Spirit and that God wants you to fast occasionally, if not more often. This leads you to a fasted life that is not given over to the foods that cause you to "live to eat" instead of eating to live.

Living to eat promotes gluttony while eating to live promotes health and vitality. Now that you've taken ground in your flesh, use this opportunity to develop better eating habits and maintain a stronger spiritual edge in your walk with God.

Don't be quick to go back to eating heavy and un-nutritional food in abundance. You conquered much and now, keep the spiritual, mental, and physical territory you took from the devil.

Before you begin eating, ponder the things the Lord revealed to you and those you received by faith. Thank God for the manifestation of those things and be mindful to do this frequently as the Holy Spirit brings those things to mind. Simply say, "Father, I thank you for _____ [healing, deliverance, victory over sickness, etc.] and continue to do so until these things manifest in your life.

Also, keep the commitments you made before God during that time. Don't be quick to forget the promise you made to God to serve Him, go to church more often, tithe more consistently, or have better character. Whatever God dealt with you about, He expects you to keep your commitment. When you do, He will keep His.

Too many believers let natural things absorb their time, talent, energy, and treasure. Little do they know that with those same God-given resources, they could be enjoying the glorious realm of God's Spirit.

The Holy Spirit desires to empower us for successful Christian living and being consistently victorious. The power God desires to release in the earth was never intended to be solely given for the use of His fivefold ministry. Yet the power comes at a price that very few are willing to pay.

I believe the Lord is raising up men and women in this hour that will pay the price and do whatever is necessary to ensure that sufficient power is available to them to accomplish His greater purposes in the earth.

You are called to be one of these powerful Christians who will receive a touch from God's glory upon your own life that comes by being a person of fasting and fasting properly.

Praying long prayers in this hour will not be enough to harness God's glorious power, you must be a person of prayer and fasting; a person who praises and worships; a person who reads and meditates upon God's Word.

Living your Christian life in this fashion is powerful and will turn your city and our entire nation around!

If you are interested in focusing your life around God, while feeding the poor, deepening your faith—read on and find out how!

Before the fast:

1. Hold the right motives. Note that fasting as a Christian means to humble yourself before Him. It is a way to glorify our Lord. Keep these aspects in mind while you fast. Don't confuse this with any other reasons for fasting such as weight loss, etc. center it around Jesus.

2. Pray before your fast. Pray, confessing every one of your sins, and invite the Holy Spirit to lead your life. Let Jesus know you wish to know him personally. Acknowledge that he lived without sin, died in our place on the cross for our sins, and rose three days later, freeing us from condemnation, and giving us His gift of eternal life. Humble yourself to ask forgiveness from everyone you have hurt; ask forgiveness from God. Forgive those who have hurt you. You do not want to enter a fast holding a grudge, carrying envy, pride, anger or hurt. The enemy will try to use those things to distract you from your fast.

3. Meditate on the gospel and on the holy traits of our Lord. These may include the ability to forgive, His strength or wisdom, His peace, the capacity to love unconditionally, etc. praise Him for these attributes! Surrender your life and thank Him for all He has done for you!

4. Determine the length of your fasting experience, whether this is for one meal, one day, three days or a week (Jesus fasted for forty days, but that is no sign that anyone else might do that). You may wish to try a shorter fast and start slowly at first if you

have not previously fasted. You can also pray and ask the Holy Spirit to reveal to you how long you should fast.
5.   Note whether you are being called to a consecration or fast. A consecration means giving up only certain types of foods. For instance, in juice fast, remove the pleasure of chewing any type of solid food, yet fruits and vegetable juices are permitted.
6.   Drink enough water to support life, since it is not a food, observing this absolute caution: in a fast, one abstains from solid and liquid "foods" – for example, fruit juices are foods – but, water is essential for life much as breathing, as one may go into a foggy mental state, then coma, and die after a mere 2 or 3 days of dehydration.

DURING THE FAST

1.   Hold morning worship. Worship Him and praise Him for His attributes. Read God's Word and meditate that God will lend me His wisdom so that I can input His Word into my life, and I can gain a fuller understanding of it. Pray for God's will to be done and for the guidance of the Holy Spirit. Ask God to lead you in spreading His glory into the world we live in.

Go for a prayer walk. Walk outside, hand in hand with nature, while noticing God's wondrous creation. Thank Him for everything He has created as you walk. Ask Him to give you a spirit of thanksgiving and appreciation.
2.   Pray for the welfare of others. Pray for church leaders to preach His Word as God intended, so that your friends and family members will grow closer to Him or accept Him into their lives; pray for government leaders to come to Him and ask Him for His will.
Fasting facilitates manifestation to prayers. Facilitates means to help bring about. The root word in facilitate is facile which means to make easy. Faculty means ability. This word thus carries the meaning of the ability to make easy. Fasting makes answers to prayer and deliverance easy.
"And Jesus said unto them, because of your unbelief: for verily I say unto you, if ye have faith as a grain of mustard seed, ye shall

say unto this mountain, remove hence to yonder place, and it shall remove, and nothing shall be impossible unto you. howbeit this kind goeth not out but *by prayer and fasting"* (Matthew 17:20,21).

Some prayers won't be answered until we fast. This is plain and directly spoken by the man who worked miracles and raised the dead. He gave the secret. When we see miracles happening in the book of Acts, we are seeing the results of fasting and praying. Spiritual power isn't free but must be desired and achieved through fasting.

"And at midnight there was a cry made, behold, the bridegroom cometh; go ye out to meet him. Then all those virgins arose and trimmed their lamps. And the foolish said unto the wise, give us of your oil; for our lamps are gone out. But the wise answered, saying, not so; lest there be not enough for us and you: but go ye rather to them that sell, and buy for yourselves" (Matthew 25:6-9).

Power for your lamps is purchased through fasting. The cost is fasting and praying, no way around it. Whatever power you have without fasting is only an imitation of the unlimited power you will have with fasting and prayer.

"Turn you at my reproof: behold, I will pour out my spirit unto you, I will make known my words unto you" (Proverbs 1:23).

Reproof is God's instructions. His Word tells how to obtain power. When we place it to the side, we miss our privilege.

"And he said unto them, can ye make the children of the bride chamber fast, while the bridegroom is with them? But the days will come, when the bridegroom shall be taken away from them, and then shall they fast in those days. And he spake also a parable unto them; no man putteth a piece of a new garment upon an old; if otherwise, then both the new maketh a rent and the piece that was taken out of the new agreth, not with the old. And no man putteth new wine into old bottles; else the new wine will burst the bottles, and be spilled, and the bottles shall perish. But new wine must be put into new bottles, and both are preserved" (Luke 5:34-38).

Fasting renews the body and restores it. Fasting is equated to having new skins or new vessels for wine to pour into. The skin

The Mystery of Fasting

represents the body that will house the power of the Spirit. New bodies represent new wine. Our bodies must be renewed to receive the renewed power of the Spirit.

"Then was Jesus led up of the spirit into the wilderness to be tempted of the devil. And when he had fasted forty days and forty nights, he was afterward an hungered" (Matthew 4:1-2).

God was led of the spirit to renew His body through fasting to obtain power, unlimited power, to be carried around and to become successful in His ministry on earth. Those who have ministries must engage fasting and prayer to prepare for power and ministry. Fasting is where we overcome the things that will attack our ministry and develop the character we need to be trusted with the power of God in order to operate with integrity and to manifest the fruit of the spirit. Fasting is seeking God with intense desire.

Fasting isn't killing the body. This word hungered reveals that the body may go days before it needs food for its survival. Many believe that fasting will kill you and cause you to become sick. We believe we must eat three square meals per day, but this isn't true. Our bodies have stored food in it enough to go days without eating; even though we may feel like we are hungry, we are not in need of food. This feeling of being hungry after 3 or 4 hours of not eating is our addiction to the food and sugar produced by it. It is of no difference than a person on drugs or narcotics that long for a fix even though their bodies don't need it. The body will go through withdrawal symptoms because of the addiction to food. The symptoms of addiction will be like that of a person on a drug. The body is saying, I need that when, in fact, it doesn't. The Bible here says Jesus was an hungered because it is revealing after forty days; Jesus' body was now in need of food. He had overcome the craving for food and lacked the food necessary for life functions. When we say we are hungry, our body is craving food but doesn't need the food.

"From that time Jesus began to preach, and to say, Repent: for the kingdom of heaven is at hand" (Matthew 4:17).

Jesus begins His ministry of preaching. His success of preaching, miracles, signs, and wonders are related to His fasting until He was hungry.

"And Jesus returned in the power of the spirit into Galilee: and there went out a fame of him through the entire region round about" (Luke 4:14).

Christ our example? He left the fast full of power and there was delivered unto Him the book of the Prophet Esaias, and when He had opened the book, He found the place where it was written, "The spirit of the Lord is upon me, because he hath anointed me to preach the gospel to the poor; he hath sent me to heal the brokenhearted, to preach deliverance to the captives, and recovering of sight to the blind, to set at liberty them that are bruised, to preach the acceptable year of the Lord" (Luke 4:17-19).

Our ministry will look like Christ's if we can do what HE did.

"And they were astonished at his doctrine: for his word was with power" (Luke 4:32).

When we use the mysteries of Scripture, they must be used properly. God gives us instructions on how to use His instruments of blessing for our lives and His glory. We must use faith, prayer, and praise in our fasting along with the insatiable hunger for God. We may labor in fasting, but we should not be overwhelmed with labor lest we miss the spiritual blessings of fasting.

"The labor of the foolish weariest every one of them, because he knoweth not how to go to the city" (Ecclesiastes 10:15).

We must know how to enter and what to use in the fast to be effective and tap the unlimited resources of power available to us. It is our inheritance. Our fast will manifest the power and blessing of our covenant rights and privileges.

"No weapon that is formed against thee shall prosper, and every tongue that shall rise against thee in judgment thou shalt condemn. This is the heritage of the servants of the lord, and their righteousness is of me, saith the Lord" (Isaiah 54:17).

This word weapon here means what is made completed and prepared for a deadly cause. This weapon isn't made to injure but to kill. It is used for violent assault and deadly offense. The weapons and devices of the devil which is used to carry out his plans to destroy and deal death blows to the children and servants of God; these weapons are instruments of death.

The Mystery of Fasting

A weapon, arm, or armament is any device that can be used with intent to inflict damage or harm. Weapons are used to increase the efficacy and efficiency of activities such as hunting, crime, law enforcement, self-defense, and warfare. In broader context, weapons may be construed to include anything used to gain a tactical, strategic, material, or mental advantage over an adversary or enemy target.

Fasting is like a fight because the devil does not want your strength to be optimal as to gain an advantage. When your spirit is full, his weapon will not prosper, succeed, experience profit, progress, or go over. In each of our lives, there are things that we encounter that seemingly have no reason for being there. We've not done anything wrong and neither are we able to find these things as part of our Biblical heritage, being associated with our new covenant with God.

Once identified, you pray in accordance with God's will and confess His Word over your life and situation, only to see things hanging on and at times even appearing to get worse. Confusion tries to set in, and you may even get to the point where you give in to these things as being God's will for your life.

Before you give in, God has a weapon for you to use that is more powerful in transforming your life than the devil would have you realize and that is the power of fasting. Fasting is a biblical mandate for you that can bring your life and thinking into greater alignment with the will of God.

What must be understood is that fasting is not just something reserved for those that profess Christ as Lord. Fasts are observed among Catholics, Jews, Muslims, Confucianists, Hindus, Buddhists, and adherents of other religious faiths. Even those that practice witchcraft fast to further their own system of belief. So, when you hear of other sectors of religion referring to fasting, it is not the same as when a believer fast.

On a personal level, people fast for various reasons and each reason can find some validity. There are times when we choose to fast because we struggle with either known or hidden sin. This could be alcoholism, cigarettes, sexual addictions, eating disorders, family problems, sickness and disease against a loved one, and even various abuses we commit or were a victim of, and we want to rid our lives of these things.

God will put us on a fast as a ministry in order to experience the breakthrough we've desired. Going through the same thing year after year can take its toll on the leadership and congregation and unless you are firmly settled in your heart that God's will must be done, you will not have the staying power to see God's vision all the way through.

Fasting also removes the devil's influence in the church and releases the power of God to be made manifest so we can experience God's open heaven over our lives, community, and city. This grace can expand to the nations of the world as we are used by God in furthering His purposes.

There are some fasts that we find ourselves on that are involuntary because of some great tragedy, some surgery we may have had or are anticipating, or because of the death of a loved one where we have no appetite for days unending. This happens especially when someone close to you passes away and your appetite leaves. No matter what the cause or reason is, fasting is always beneficial to us as believers. As powerful as the results are, many people still do not fast because of the inconvenience it places on their fleshly nature. During the time of fasting, especially in the initial days, until your flesh is submissive to your spirit, you're reminded of how hungry you are and how bad you need food to sustain your life.

The fact is that fasting is one of the activities the enemy fights against more than any other as it secures victory for you that cannot be won in any other way.

NOTE: Fasting is not the only weapons of deadly power but also your tongue.

The Tongue: One of Man's Most Dangerous Weapons

It is not without significance that two of the Ten Commandments deal with speech—taking the name of God in vain and bearing false witness against another person (Ex. 20:7, 16).

Similarly, in the Sermon on the Mount, Jesus warned against the abuse of the tongue in "swearing falsely" (Matthew 5:33-37). Elsewhere, Jesus Christ gave a stern warning regarding the unseemly language that sometimes proceeds from a person's

The Mystery of Fasting

mouth (Matthew 12:36-37). The way one talks is a very revealing index to their character. The Scriptures describe different kinds of "tongues" (speech). The word tongue here in Hebrew is **"lashown"**. It means a malignant tongue or words, a slander, or enchanter. Now the word enchanter is interesting because it means sorcery.

Lashown here is words which are thoughts that come directly from demons and familiar spirits. These words are deadly and will spread in rapid uncontrolled ways throughout our lives with the ability and purpose to cause death. These words will come from folks being used by familiar spirits, (I.e. evil spirits).

When the fast is over, you must still represent your Lord well. Some of us need to fast to get control of our tongue as the things we say are destroying us and those around us.

Neglecting to be victorious over our words and choosing to only speak those things that will edify and encourage others causes people to lose respect for us and the very gospel we're trying to get them to accept. They lose respect for the message and the One the message is all about—Jesus!

The principle is: during the fast, we watch what goes into our bodies [or what we don't allow in]. After the fast is over, we must watch what comes out. This becomes more important than ever as you don't want to lose the ground you gained through fasting by not making your

speech a priority.

Also referring to the use of the tongue, James 3 says in the NKJV:

"[1] My brethren, let not many of you become teachers, knowing that we shall receive a stricter judgment. [2] For we all stumble in many things. If anyone does not stumble in word, he is a perfect man, able also to bridle the whole body. [3] Indeed, we put bits in horses' mouths that they may obey us, and we turn their whole body. [4] Look also at ships: although they are so large and are driven by fierce winds, they are turned by a very small rudder wherever the pilot desires. [5] Even so the tongue is a little member and boasts great things. See how a little fire kindles a great forest!

[6] And the tongue is a fire, a world of iniquity. The tongue is so set among our members that it defiles the whole body and sets on

fire the course of nature; and it is set on fire by hell. [7] For every kind of beast and bird, of reptile and creature of the sea, is tamed and has been tamed by mankind. [8] But no man can tame the tongue. It is an unruly evil, full of deadly poison. [9] With it we bless our God and Father, and with it we curse men, who have been made in the similitude of God. [10] Out of the same mouth proceed blessing and cursing. My brethren, these things ought not to be so."

You must learn to control your tongue. There must come a time in your life when you don't say everything that comes to mind. You must select and use words carefully if you are going to be considered by God as being perfect or mature.

Watching our tongues takes learning to speak in agreement with the fruit of the Spirit where we must speak in love and speak with kindness. This means we should consider the words we say and speak while being controlled by the Spirit of God.

To speak without considering the feelings of the other person and the potential long-term damage can bring heartache in the relationship for months and even years.

Verse 6 says, **the tongue is a world of iniquity. Iniquity is wickedness, evil, sin, and injustice.**

This is how God views the tongue of man until it is fully given over to the Holy Spirit. He's saying that this may not be an easy thing, but it can be done with effort and by your obedience to Him.

Each of us at some point has said things that we have had to apologize for. This happens not only on the job and in school, but in our homes where those we love the most, we take for granted. Once something is spoken, as much as you want to, you cannot recant it.

Ephesians 4:29 says, "Let no corrupt word proceed out of your mouth." This is so important to God that the Bible says in Matthew 12:36, "For every idle word men may speak, they will give account of it in the day of judgment."

You must decide to do this and the way it will happen is through humbling yourself and fasting unto God.

10

MANIFESTATIONS OF THE SONS OF GOD

[18] "for I reckon that the sufferings of this present time are not worthy to be compared with the glory which shall be revealed in us.
[19] *For the earnest expectation of the creature waiteth for the manifestation of the sons of God"* (Romans 8:18-19).
The sacrifice of fasting can compare to the glory of God that will be revealed and showcased in your life.
God wants to showcase you.
He desires you be a light to bring light to others. To bring liberty. Yes, feeding the hungry is good, and all services provided.
But we have begun to substitute secondary things as the priority for the power of God to deliver and set free. We are to operate at the same level as Christ did.
Communities are groaning, neighborhoods are groaning, families are groaning, loved ones are groaning, but we are powerless.
This is a call by God for the manifestation of the sons of God to manifest because all of creation is waiting.
The flesh is miserable while becoming subject to God, therefore the subject of fasting isn't prevalent in the church toady as in the apostolic days.

In fact, Muslims fast more than we do, and religions do it without the promises God gives us today.

"[12] Verily, verily, I say unto you, he that believeth on me, the works that I do shall he do also; and greater works than these shall he do; because I go unto my father.

[13] And whatsoever ye shall ask in my name, that will I do, that the father may be glorified in the son.

[14] If ye shall ask any thing in my name, I will do it" (John 14:12-14).

This scripture isn't speaking about prayer here but doing the works of Christ on earth in his name.

This is us demanding the devil to lose and let go of God's folks.

This is healing and being a wonder through the power of the spirit.

We are told to do the same works Christ did. But Christ laid the foundation of prayer before he walked in his ministry.

Yes, Jesus turned water into wine before his ministry started.

This wasn't the beginning of his ministry. Remember he asked his mother why she is calling him before his time.

Many witnessed some of the powers God has placed on our lives and believe that's it, that's all. But know your true ministry will start when we would have done what Jesus did and fasted.

Many have given themselves over to the things of gimmicks in the house of God and manipulation to control the minds of folks because they have neglected the power of God to do Christ's kind of work.

Fasting is for a deeper level of purification and sanctification in order to experience the wonders of God and his power to fully manifest his gifts in our lives for service unto him.

"[15] blow the trumpet in Zion, sanctify a fast, call a solemn assembly: [16] Gather the people, sanctify the congregation, assemble the elders, gather the children, and those that suck the breasts: let the bridegroom go forth of his chamber, and the bride out of her closet.

[17] Let the priests, the ministers of the lord, weep between the porch and the altar, and let them say, spare thy people, o lord, and give not thine heritage to reproach, that the heathen should rule over them: wherefore

The Mystery of Fasting

should they say among the people, where is their God?
[18] Then will the lord be jealous for his land and pity his people.
[19] Yea, the lord will answer and say unto his people, behold, I will send you corn, and wine, and oil, and ye shall be satisfied therewith: and I will no more make you a reproach among the heathen" (Joel 2:15-19). When you fast, God becomes moved to do something. In the verse above, he turns their poverty into rich prosperity.

God said, for I may do this thing for you.

"[23] be glad then, ye children of Zion, and rejoice in the lord your God: for he hath given you the former rain moderately, and he will cause to come down for you the rain, the former rain, and the latter rain in the first month.
[24] And the floors shall be full of wheat, and the fats shall overflow with wine and oil.
[25] And I will restore to you the years that the locust hath eaten, the cankerworm, and the caterpillar, and the palmerworm, my great army which I sent among you.
[26] And ye shall eat in plenty, and be satisfied, and praise the name of the lord your God, that hath dealt wondrously with you: and my people shall never be ashamed.
27]*And ye shall know that I am in the midst of Israel, and that I am the lord your God, and none else: and my people shall never be ashamed"* (Joel 2:23-27).

For their fasting God is saying, I am going to restore all that has been taken from you.

He says, rejoice I am turning your poverty to prosperity.
In other words, I'm delivering you from oppression of the devil.
But this isn't the part I want to get to.

And it shall come to pass, that whosoever shall call on the name of the lord shall be delivered: for in mount Zion and in Jerusalem shall be deliverance, as the lord hath said, and in the remnant whom the lord shall call" (Joel 2:32).

This is the part where it says, I will pour out my spirit.
So, the fast does two things, it will deliver you from oppression. And in addition to delivering, it will cause you to become and carry the manifestation of the spirit to deliver others.

"and, behold, I send the promise of my father upon you: but tarry ye in the city of Jerusalem, until ye be endued with power from on high" (Luke 24:49).

We are instructed to be endued which means to be enveloped or clothed with the power of Christ which means the anointed one. The apostles fasted. In fact, they felt it necessary to pray and fast before sending out new elders to manifest the works of Christ.

"[22] Confirming the souls of the disciples, and exhorting them to continue in the faith, and that we must through much tribulation enter into the kingdom of God.
[23] *And when they had ordained them elders in every church, and had prayed with fasting, they commended them to the lord, on whom they believed"* (acts 14:22-23).

Paul fasted

"in weariness and painfulness, in watchings often, in hunger and thirst, in fasting often, in cold and nakedness" (2 Corinthians 11:27).

He tells to follow his example

"Brethren be followers together of me and mark them which walk so as ye have us for an ensample" (Philippians 3:17).

Paul in this verse he fasted often

Fasting is a travail that births power, prophecies, miracles, and the full manifestation of God on our lives.

"how God anointed Jesus of Nazareth with the holy ghost and with power: who went about doing good and healing all that were oppressed of the devil; for God was with him" (Acts 10:38).

Jesus fasted and these things were present in his life. We must fast to do the works of Christ. The world is groaning for us.

"But as for me, when they were sick, my clothing was sackcloth: I humbled my soul with fasting; and my prayer returned into mine own bosom" (Psalm 35:13).

David fasted. This was how he received the visions of the messiah and his death and resurrection years before it happened.

Jesus desires to reveal the eternal mysteries to us but we must fast and sacrifice for these deeper revelations of God.

You don't just wish and hope to find out the deeper things of God. You gain access to them through the foolishness OF FASTING.

The Mystery of Fasting

"[2] The LORD shall send the rod of thy strength out of Zion: rule thou in the midst of thine enemies.
[3] Thy people shall be willing in the day of thy power, in the beauties of holiness from the womb of the morning: thou hast the dew of thy youth" (Psalm 110:2-3).

We are to experience supernatural power of dominion over all life's situations. We are to rule amid our enemies.

They will watch but can't stop the rulership. It is now time for the manifest sons of God to rule as Christ ruled on earth.

John 1:4

"[4] *in him was life; and the life was the light of men.*
*[5] and the light shineth in darkness; and the darkness comprehended it no*t" (John 1:4-5).

God desires you to be illuminated. Your light will dispel the darkness.

Darkness cannot overpower you. When you walk to do ministry, your light will dispel darkness,

When sickness sees you coming, it will leave. When those demons saw Jesus coming, they asked, what have we to do with you? Please don't cast us out before our time. They recognized his light.

Demons recognize your light and get up.

Your light will put to flight the assault of demons oppressing you and other people.

"*[6] Is not this the fast that I have chosen? to loose the bands of wickedness, to undo the heavy burdens, and to let the oppressed go free, and that ye*

break every yoke?
[7]Is it not to deal thy bread to the hungry, and that thou bring the poor *that are cast out to thy house? when thou seest the naked, that thou cover him; and that thou hide not thyself from thine own flesh?*
[8] Then shall thy light break forth as the morning, and thine health shall spring forth speedily: and thy righteousness shall go before thee; the glory of the LORD shall be thy rereward" (Isaiah 58:6-8).

Fasting brings forth light that's illumination and revelation from God. The fast that God calls is for the sake of ministry. Empowerment for ministry. Verse 6 says to loose the bands, lift the burdens off folk, and deliver the oppressed. Then it is to give...Fasting is about giving instead of receiving. But when we fast with deliverance for others in mind, verse 8 says, then shall light break forth. God will give revelation, deliver you, and make you whole to be a light to the nations. The glory or power of God shall be your reward for the fasting.

CONCLUSION

As I tell everyone who will listen: Fasting is a weapon in a Christian's spiritual armory, you need to know WHEN to use it. It is neither the equivalent of a B-B gun nor a .22 caliber bullet in power, nor even the most significant military artillery round. Instead, it is the equivalent of a spiritual NUCLEAR WARHEAD. You need to learn that it IS a weapon that is potent, and you need to learn how to use it when it's time to use it wisely.

Personal Fasting Record

The Mystery of Fasting

Personal Fasting Record

Nathaniel McNeil

Personal Fasting Record

Nathaniel McNeil

Personal Fasting Record

Personal Fasting Record

Nathaniel McNeil

Personal Fasting Record

Personal Fasting Record

Nathaniel McNeil

Personal Fasting Record

Personal Fasting Record

Nathaniel McNeil

Personal Fasting Record

Personal Fasting Record

Nathaniel McNeil

Personal Fasting Record

Personal Fasting Record

Nathaniel McNeil

Personal Fasting Record

Personal Fasting Record

Nathaniel McNeil

Personal Fasting Record

Personal Fasting Record

Nathaniel McNeil

Personal Fasting Record

For speaking engagements, conferences, revivals and seminars contact Nathaniel mcneil by email at bishopnmcneil@icloud .com

www.ingramcontent.com/pod-product-compliance
Lightning Source LLC
Chambersburg PA
CBHW052136110526
44591CB00012B/1750